GORDON BANKS

BANKS

– A BIOGRAPHY –

GORDON BANKS
– A BIOGRAPHY –

Jim Morris

AMBERLEY

First published 2013

Amberley Publishing
The Hill, Stroud
Gloucestershire, GL5 4EP

www.amberley-books.com

British Library Cataloguing in Publication Data.
A catalogue record for this book is available from the British Library.

ISBN 978 1 4456 1655 1 (print)
ISBN 978 1 4456 1674 2 (ebook)

Typeset in 10.5pt on 13pt Sabon.
Typesetting and Origination by Amberley Publishing.
Printed in the UK.

Contents

Prologue

We'd had our colour television for a few months and it made all the difference to watching the football. I can remember many a game in black and white where you couldn't tell the teams apart, but the advert told us that 'With colour it comes alive!' And it did.

Saturday night, after the players had made their way into the bath and off home, *Match of the Day* would crash into the lounge with Kenneth Wolstenholme, David Coleman, Barry Davies and the rest. On Sunday afternoons, we had *The Big Match* on ITV with Brian Moore featuring a significant game from London, and perhaps a snippit of Hugh Johns from the Midlands, or perhaps Keith Macklin from Yorkshire Television. Alternatively, Brian might say, 'The pictures are from Granada Television and your commentator is Gerald Sinstadt,' and off we'd go to Manchester or Liverpool – need one say more.

And it was on a Saturday afternoon in late October 1972 that Anfield and League leaders Liverpool played host to Stoke City. Liverpool took to the field in their familiar all-red strip, and Stoke in their second strip of white shirts and black shorts. In those pre-Premier League days, a team earned two points for a win and one point for a draw, and Liverpool, on nineteen points, were top of the First Division, one point ahead of Arsenal with a game in hand (i.e. Arsenal had played one more match than Liverpool). Stoke City were eighteenth, but that might not be as bad as it seems because they were two places above Manchester United and three places above Manchester City!

The referee that afternoon was Roger Kirkpatrick (aka Mr Kirk-Pickwick), who could run faster backwards than he could forwards. A great sport, sadly no longer with us.

Liverpool dictated play early on with Emlyn Hughes stretching Gordon Banks. Kevin Keegan was dominant, as was Ian Callaghan, with left-back Alec Lindsay frequently overlapping down the left flank, and fellow full-back Chris Lawler joining in the attack on the right. In fact, it was Chris who produced the best piece of action in the first half. Alec Lindsay's left foot (the one Bill Shankly said he 'could peel an orange with') crossed a high ball to the far side of the 6-yard box. Chris Lawler jumped to head the ball in unison with Peter Cormack – Alan Bloor was defending for the visitors – but the ball fell loose and Chris, at ninety degrees to goal on the angle of the 6-yard box, chipped the ball with the outside of his right foot – an up and under. It was looking like it would creep in just under the bar on its way down: 'That was Lawler, and he's there again. And he almost made it, if it hadn't been Gordon Banks in that goal, he would've done!'

Gordon finished up in a bit of a heap inside his own net, but the ball didn't.

At the other end, Ray Clemence in the Liverpool goal – in front of the mighty Kop – had little to do (that season he kept twenty-six clean sheets), but a free-kick on the halfway line by John Marsh travelled deep into Liverpool's 18-yard box, where Jimmy Greenhoff headed it down to a Stoke newcomer, one Geoff Hurst, on the 6-yard line. Geoff first tried with his left foot, which was blocked – he had Chris Lawler, Alec Lindsay and Emlyn Hughes surrounding him – but still managed to get the ball onto his right foot for a second attempt. This time it hit the bar and bounced straight out and onto Jimmy Greenhoff's head. Stoke scored, and the first half ended with Stoke City a goal up.

At the start of the second half, Gordon ran to his goal at the Kop end and was given a sporting reception by the Liverpool army – and, not for the first time, they were great. It wasn't long before Liverpool's Steve Heighway was storming down the left and crossed to the far post. Peter Cormack headed back across the mouth of the goal to Phil Boersma, who was about 6 feet from the goal but off balance, and the ball went screeching over the bar.

In those days, a goalkeeper was restricted to four paces holding the ball. Often they would dribble the ball before kicking or throwing a clearance. If they went to throw the ball and changed their mind, preferring the big boot up the field, then they might lose count of how many paces they had taken. Gordon gave away an indirect free-kick for such an offence. Alec Lindsay side-footed the ball to Emlyn Hughes, who controlled the ball with his left foot as he ran forward. The defensive wall Stoke had created dispersed, Gordon was on the 6-yard line while Emlyn was on the 18-yard line – he struck the ball with his right foot, it took a deflection and was in the back of the Stoke net before anyone realised the shot had been made.

Liverpool maintained the pressure looking for the winner. Another Steve Heighway cross found Peter Cormack without a Stoke defender near him, and he almost had a free header but it went straight into Gordon's arms.

Kevin Keegan was nearly on the end of a near perfect defence-splitting pass from Tommy Smith, before Denis Smith and Mike Pejic put an unceremonious halt to him, just outside the 18-yard box. Stoke City's five-man wall stood in keen anticipation, and Gordon was a foot or two off his line. Alec Lindsay, with his match nonchalance, rolled the ball forward for Tommy Smith to crack at goal – Gordon couldn't hold it and Phil Boersma ran in to follow up, but he crashed it wide. It was looking as though the points would be shared, but after forty seconds of injury time, Steve Heighway picked the ball up just inside Stoke's half. He was away and rode the tackle by Eric Skeels, or seemed to, before Jimmy Robertson intercepted to pass the ball back to Gordon – in those days when the defender passed back to the goalkeeper he was permitted to pick it up – but just as Jimmy played the ball, Mr K blew the whistle for a foul. It seemed as though it was a fair piece of play, and the Stoke players felt it was late for the ref to stop play. Mr K had waved play on after Eric Skeels' challenge on Steve Heighway, but did he blow a little late for this later challenge? It did seem a harsh decision. Steve Heighway had stumbled a bit, but didn't look as though he felt he'd been fouled. But like all professionals, they tended to get on with the game. Emlyn Hughes rolled the ball off to Ian Callaghan, who hit it with all his might from about 30 yards. It hit a couple of players but managed to find the back of the net, and it looked like Liverpool would be taking the points.

Half a minute after the kick-off, Mr K blew for full-time. Before Gerald Sinstadt had finished the commentary, Ray Clemence was calming Gordon down – he'd been having a word with the referee, who'd waved him clear. That small altercation took place just inside the Liverpool half of the field, so Gordon had run from his goal to discuss this with Mr K. It seemed that late decision troubled him, as did the earlier decision about his steps – though the latter seems fair when watching the game now.

During the game, Gordon had picked up a bit of a knock and an appointment was made for the following day with the club physiotherapist, after which he was keen to get home to his Sunday dinner. He drove a Ford Consul, which was a nippy car for its size, but the trip was slowed by another driver stuck behind a lorry. Gordon pulled out to overtake – not the wisest thing to do because he put himself on a collision course with a van. He said years later he'd been preoccupied with the controversies in the match the day before.

Twenty-eight-year-old Roger Peake and his wife Glynnis, who was two years younger, together with their three-year-old son Andrew, were travelling along at something like 40 miles an hour in their Austin A35 van when Gordon pulled out in front of them. When you can see a road accident about to happen, one of two things are possible – either the mind completely edits it from consciousness so recollection of the event subsides into the subconscious, or the details stay with you. What seemed to happen to Gordon was the former. Mr Peake was able to take some evasive action and later said he pulled onto the grass verge. An unconfirmed report said the brakes on Gordon's car were questionable. The offside wing of the car took the brunt of the impact and the windscreen shattered – it has also been recorded that the rear-view mirror on the windscreen shattered with the impact. Mr and Mrs Peake and their son were not seriously injured, though Gordon heard a child crying and his first thought was for him.

It had been drizzling that day, which made the road slippery, but the accident happened in broad daylight. A Mr Lawrence Bond was passing and stopped to see what help he could give. Gordon had been knocked temporarily senseless by the accident, and despite his razor-sharp eyesight and his legendary reactions, he was unable to explain the accident – but the events of the day before were at the front of his mind.

In those days seatbelts were not a legal requirement, and he'd not been wearing his. With a head-on crash at 40 miles an hour the body will lunge forward at terrific speed, and but for the grace of God we would have lost Gordon completely. He did lose the sight of an eye, and his days at the top in soccer were over.

At the time he was reigning Footballer of the Year, and had been awarded the OBE in 1970. Football was to lose one of its greatest players and Stoke City lost yet another legend – the previous one was Sir Stanley Matthews, the wizard of the dribble. Gordon was the wizard of the right dive, and at full stretch could get a palm up and push the ball over the bar to stop a certain master from Brazil. He could also stop a stinging penalty from Geoff Hurst – then of West Ham United – and put Stoke City into a Wembley cup final.

So when will history tell us the Hand of God made its debut? In 1986, or much earlier?

Introduction

Gordon Banks was born on 30 December 1937 and became widely regarded as the best goalkeeper England ever produced, and among the best the world has ever seen. The debate really should end there as his main rivals to the world crown include the Russian Lev Yashin, Italy's Dino Zoff and the West German Sepp Maier. Far more of Gordon's heroics are available on DVD or online, and not so much of the others; so it's not possible for the armchair fan to compare, and there seems little point – let's just call him England's greatest.

Nellie (Ellen) Yates accepted the marriage proposal of Thomas Banks, and they married in Sheffield in the autumn of 1927 – Mr Banks senior worked in the steel industry. They had four sons: John (Jack) was born in 1931, Michael followed the next year, David was born in 1934 and Gordon appeared in 1937 – but only just. The family lived in Arthur Road in Sheffield, but they later moved to Ferrars Road in the Tinsley district. By the early 1950s, they were in Catcliffe, where Mr Banks also ran a betting shop (not legal at the time, but that's something I'll come back to).

Gordon was passionate about his football and would play in any position simply to 'get a game'. He finished up more often than not as goalkeeper: 'No one wanted to play in goal and the game could never start' so he agreed to 'go in for one and then we'd take it in turns'.

He played for Tinsley County School while a pupil there, and represented Sheffield Boys twice before he was dispensed with quite abruptly and with no explanation. Any hope he might have had for football to be a career seemed like it would die early. When he left school (at fifteen in those days), Gordon worked as a coal bagger for a local coal merchant, which actually rendered him too exhausted to play football. His brother managed to get him into the building industry and he commenced an apprenticeship as a bricklayer; he later said he would have been content to have stayed at this.

But he remained passionate about his football, and it didn't take much to persuade him to join Millspaugh FC – a steelworks team – after he had turned out to watch them one Saturday and their goalkeeper hadn't turned up.

While with Millspaugh, he was spotted and asked to trial for a team in a higher League – Rawmarsh Welfare, a colliery team. But in his first game they were beaten 12-2 by a high-grade side called Stocksbridge Works. The following week, the defeat was 3-1. The week after that he was without a football club as the manager didn't invite him to play for them again, and he thought that when he returned to Millspaugh that might have been the only excursion up in quality he was to make.

But a scout for Chesterfield liked Gordon's football and he joined the club as a part-time professional – by now he had turned eighteen. Gordon was initially paid by the game (£2), but when he received wages it only went up to £3 a week – this was in the days when there was a maximum wage for footballers. His manager at Chesterfield was Ted Davison, who'd been a goalkeeper himself, so he recognised Gordon's qualities as soon as he saw him play. The youth team in which Gordon was a budding star reached the final of the FA Youth Cup in 1956, where they lost to a Manchester United youth side – the Busby Babes. Gordon made his League debut in the Third Division for Chesterfield at the end of November 1958 in a 2-2 draw at home to Colchester United. His days at Chesterfield were better than that with Rawmarsh Welfare – in his second game against Carlisle United he kept a clean sheet – so his future in the game began to look more settled.

It was with the Royal Signals Regiment that he did his two years of National Service. With Gordon in goal, his regiment won the Rhine Cup, and word of this reached the English shores. But far more importantly, he met a young lady at a dance, Ursula Weimann, who he was to marry, and the new Mr and Mrs Banks had three children; Robert in 1958, Wendy in 1963 and Julia in 1969. Grandchildren eventually followed.

But ten years before Julia made her appearance, Gordon, who'd only made twenty-three appearances for Chesterfield, joined Leicester City, a first-division club, for a £7,000 transfer fee. Leicester rode high in the First Division and they were to reach two FA Cup finals during the early 1960s – in 1961 when they were beaten 2-0 by the double-winning Tottenham Hotspur, followed by another disappointment two years later when Manchester United won 3-1. Leicester's progression through the rounds seemed far more straightforward in 1963, but in 1961 they had a replay in the fifth round against Birmingham City, and again in the sixth round against Barnsley (who didn't have floodlights so the game was played on a weekday afternoon); in the semi-final, Leicester managed to beat Sheffield United at a second replay. The football season was long and gruelling, with penalty shoot-outs a thing of the distant future.

Leicester were under the management of Matt Gillies, who was a leading tactician of his day, one might even say a pioneering tactician. He would juggle the role and number of the team, so sides quickly got the message to mark the man and not the number on his shirt.

But Leicester did win a domestic trophy – the fledgling and initially unpopular Football League Cup in 1964 – when, over two legs, at home and away, they beat Stoke City 4-3. Gordon was later to become a Football League Cup winner in 1972 with his opponents of that day.

Leicester City enjoyed mid-table status in the First Division, and in April 1963 Gordon made his international debut against Scotland at Wembley, sadly without keeping a clean sheet; the Scots won 2-1. But Mr (as he was then) Alf Ramsey knew quality when he saw it, and this defeat came a mere six months into Mr Ramsey's tenure as England manager. Ron Springett, the Sheffield Wednesday goalkeeper, shared the honour as England's goalkeeper, but Gordon soon became the first choice and when Mr Ramsey announced his squad for the 1966 World Cup, the goalkeeper's No. 1 jersey went to Gordon Banks.

It has been said that the 1953 6-3 defeat of Hungary at Wembley was the end of England's world domination, but in 1966 England became World Champions, so perhaps it wasn't quite the end.

England finished up in third place in the 1968 European Championships, and in 1970 were knocked out by West Germany in the quarter-finals of the World Cup in Mexico – Gordon didn't play in that particular match and I'll discuss this in more detail later. In the group rounds he did make what one might regard as the save of the tournament against Pelé in England's match with Brazil – others have called it the save of the century. England were to perform poorly in the 1972 European Championships, and were again knocked out by West Germany.

But on the domestic front, Gordon had made 293 appearances at Leicester when he was transferred to Stoke City for £52,000 in April 1967, and his career there reached its peak in 1972 when they won the Football League Cup final (by now a one-match affair at Wembley), beating Chelsea 2-1. This cup campaign had many notable highlights, but in Gordon's view a save against West Ham in the semi-final – a Geoff Hurst penalty – was his own personal favourite.

It was with Stoke City that his footballing career came to an unfortunate end. Following his road accident, despite a lot of hard training, it became clear that his impaired vision might not serve the demands made by the First Division, and in 1973 he announced his retirement from top-class football. He did play later in America, where he was judged to be on top of his form.

Gordon started coaching and later took the job of manager for Telford United, but after a very short though not unsuccessful time, he was dismissed – this came after he'd been away for surgery on his hip and the caretaker rather let the side down. Gordon realised the job of manager was not just to bark at the players on a Saturday afternoon, and much work was done behind the scenes. When the end came he felt it was a kick in the teeth, and it upset him to such a degree he didn't enter football management again.

He went into the business world, and for a number of years was in partnership in Leicester. Though it didn't work out, it seemed good while it lasted – or good for the bulk of its life.

The active life of a goalkeeper is generally a bit longer than an outfield player, and his successor for England (strictly Ray Clemence but) Peter Shilton went on to win 125 caps and was an England goalkeeper until the age of forty, so in Gordon's career there is a large deficit when one can only think about what might have been.

In all, Gordon played 703 professional games, which includes seventy-three for England, and he kept a clean sheet for his country no fewer than thirty-five times. Undoubtedly, he would have had a good few seasons more to play, and he has said that in 1970, two years before the accident, he was at his peak physically and mentally.

In later years as more interest has been shown in football history, many questions have been asked about the 1970 World Cup finals in Mexico. Peter Bonetti deputised for Gordon in the quarter-final match against West Germany. England went two goals up before the Germans fought back – Peter was unlucky with both the first and then the equaliser and was the target of unfair criticism. Gordon had eaten the same meal as the other England players the night before but had an acute bout of food poisoning that laid him up – only a few of the others had minor, if any, symptoms.

With that and Bobby Moore being accused of the theft of a bracelet, one would be forgiven for thinking the two might be linked. Bobby was exonerated and the squad put that episode behind them. But what of Gordon Banks? Peter Bonetti was a world-class goalkeeper and a worthy stand-in, but with so many in the squad eating the same food and the only person to be struck down ... one has to wonder. Initially he thought it was just an unfortunate turn of events, but over the years he has come to question the episode, and if enough people ask the same question one might start to ask, what is the truth?

So the story of 'Banks of England' is well worth reconsidering, but this book is not a consideration of any 'conspiracy theory', rather it is a celebration of a great sportsman. It is true to say that he faced the greatest footballers in the world, but it might be more relevant to say that the greatest footballers in the world faced him.

1

Through the Teens

Life in the Banks household was of the usual pressures of kids growing up; the war came, was won, and went, and Britain faced many years of austerity as it tried to pick itself up socially and economically. Football played a large part in the hearts of both boys and men, with record numbers going through the turnstiles each week. During the week there was discussion about the game that had passed, and the game that was yet to come. Football was the national sport and something 'Joe Public' could be passionate about.

There was televised football, but precious little of it; most of it was on the radio – or wireless as it was then called. *Match of the Day* and *The Big Match* were still years away, and it wasn't until the mid- to late 1980s that live League football was on the box. And an entire channel just for football relayed from an object in the sky was still quite firmly in the hands of H. G. Wells. But 1938 saw the first televised FA Cup final, so things were beginning to move towards the armchair – the fact that it all went too far and led to the pundits on the television telling us what we'd just seen was something we'd have to endure.

Ferrars Road in Tinsley, Sheffield, was the headquarters of the Thomas and Ellen Banks empire and their four boys, Jack (John), Michael, David and Gordon. In common with most other families in the country, although it sounds as though 'the North' had it much tougher, there was a chronic shortage of money and therefore a barren standard of living. Sheffield had the steel industry, which was a major employer. But as the country was football mad, it's no surprise that other sports were also on their uppers. So gambling was something a lot of northern men, and lots of southern ones too, liked to indulge in. It was only possible to bet at official functions, so dog tracks and horse-racing tracks were the main venues for the betting fraternity. But the British spirit saw more than just trains go underground, as more and more illegal bookies' shops began to appear. Finally it was brought out into the open, as a law against some activities doesn't necessarily stop them, it just gives the country an unenforceable law.

Thomas Banks was one who operated a book and took small bets from a small circle of clients. Mr Banks could also include farming and lorry transport among his many attempts to provide a better standard of living to his family. To say these early betting shops were actually shops would be misleading: it wasn't necessarily a proper shop with open or closed on the door, and many a 'book' would be at a workplace, or in the saloon bar of a pub, and no doubt countless other places too. Gordon's father stayed mainly on the racing tracks as the 'anti-betting' laws were rigorously applied in Sheffield in those days. But it had gone on for a number of years and it did help Mr and Mrs Banks' budget.

The family moved to the small mining village of Catcliffe, just outside Sheffield, where Mr Banks opened his bookie's shop. The penalties were stiff if the law did descend, but Mr Banks had a drinking buddy who knew when the police were likely to raid – he was one of them! It was a risk still and the penalty was a fine of something like £40, which was a huge amount of money in those days, but this gives some idea of the benefits. Catcliffe falls in the metropolitan borough of Rotherham, and in those days the police forces of Sheffield and Rotherham were separate. In Sheffield, the anti-betting laws were more rigorously enforced than they were outside its boundaries, and it wasn't unheard of for one of Mr Banks' former clients to take a taxi out to Catcliffe to put a bet on!

All these decades later in the Catcliffe Arches a Mr Banks still makes a living, but now selling pottery – this is Gordon's nephew. The Catcliffe Arches took the railway line from east to west, and just to the north of the railway line was a farm. Gordon laughs as he remembers the chickens occasionally wandering down under the arch which was Mr Banks' 'betting shop' – anything to help the family budget – and laying eggs. His father was quite an entrepreneur.

Unfortunately, in any society there will be those who want the quick way to riches by taking someone else's. In those days crime was quite different to what it is today, insofar as theft went. Wages snatches – wages were mostly paid in cash – were common, as were armed bank robberies; but one thing that has remained with us, sadly, is those who use gratuitous violence when a few thumps would do the job. It wouldn't have been difficult to work out that the bookies were usually on the profitable end of a flutter, and a shop might take in a good bit of cash with a good day's racing. And one day when Jack Banks had left the shop and was on his way home, he was attacked and robbed.

Jack had never enjoyed good health, and this was something the robbers would have been aware of quite quickly; he walked with a stick and was only about 5 feet in height. In his autobiography, Gordon has described his brother's health problems. The robbers beat Jack up fairly badly and he was in hospital for a prolonged period – and I gather the robbers went to prison for a long period. But anyone who has had this sort of trauma will tell you that the punishment doesn't compensate for the pain you see your loved one endure.

Jack was to die young, though this seems to be because of his general health. But Gordon speaks fondly of him even these many years later.

Michael and David settled to life away from the pressures and pleasures of professional football. It had been David who got Gordon the job as apprentice bricklayer, but he was supportive of his footballing and his brothers and dad would watch him at Chesterfield and all through. David remembered Gordon playing as centre-forward too, and told a story of him giving the ball a good 'crack' but it going over the bar and breaking a house window. As the years caught up, David, the more extraverted of his brothers, began to forget little things and show difficulty in keeping up with conversations. Sadly, his decline continued and he was diagnosed as suffering from Alzheimer's disease – on his death Gordon became involved in the Staffordshire branch of the Alzheimer's Society. Michael Banks worked with his father when he tried, but didn't quite succeed, in the haulage business; later, Michael joined British Rail.

2

Shaping the Mould

No matter what one does, from whatever walk of life, there will always be particular things, events or people who will contribute to 'moulding one's shape'. They may be parents or teachers, or anyone looked up to in awe in one's early years. These folk generally have a major influence on our lives because they are a huge part of it. But as development moves on, so do the people who influence us change – and I make this a deliberate simplification. And there is a difference between moulding one's shape and folk who influence. Often an interest in something like football will lead to an admiration of particular players, and thereafter the influence mechanisms start to work. The people we learn from are not always the people who teach us.

These days there are coaches in football who specialise in goalkeeping, and with the technology now available one can watch, countless times, a particular piece of play on video or other apparatus. I'm not talking necessarily of the television pundits who tell us what we have just seen in a recording, but in researching this book I considered some of what Gordon had said and written (I'll discuss his writing later), and then applied it to recordings of his performance, easily available on the internet or on video. As a consequence, I can begin to see the unique challenges presented to a goalkeeper, and how their role in the team is so different to their teammates.

I think it was in Bob Wilson's autobiography I learnt that at the end of a game, while the outfield players are physically exhausted, it's the mental exhaustion that takes its toll on goalkeepers. I can remember quite clearly Pat Jennings describing Bob's coaching skills. He specialised in goalkeeping and was so good that he enjoyed a good few extra years in his career. If one takes all of the top goalkeepers of the post-war period, they have to be considered as pioneers in an art.

Then there is the science side of it, not to mention the psychological. There is also the downright brute force of two men jumping – one to catch a ball or propel it one way, and the other to get his head to the ball and propel it the other, and if the ball happens to be in the goalkeeper's hands when the opposing forward collides with him and goalkeeper and ball end up in a crumpled heap, then that's all part of it. It might not even be one of the opposing side's players.

Bringing things a bit closer to the ground, a sharp volley can see a goalkeeper fly across the goalmouth to just get his fingertips to a ball and tip it wide or over. Then comes the landing one hopes is graceful and painless – and not an unfortunate landing in which there is a collision with another player or the goalpost.

And there's the ground-level stuff where the ball comes in at foot level. A lot of football takes place down there, so the goalkeeper has to get his hands down to the ground and probably his upper body in accompaniment, with heavy football boots flailing and slicing everywhere – the boots perhaps of teammates as well as the opposition. It is therefore small wonder that there are now coaches who specialise in goalkeeping, and the younger goalkeepers can study Gordon's and other top goalkeepers' application of the job.

It's of no surprise then that over the years he copped a few boots, head collisions and the like (or dislike!), but one needs to consider just how Gordon learnt his trade.

By watching other goalkeepers for a start. But in his early years, Gordon couldn't afford to go to see a football match each week – Sheffield had the two teams: United and Wednesday, though he never had any strong affiliation to either. United's Ted Burgin was one goalkeeper Gordon was to refer to, and Wednesday's David McIntosh was also an early influence. But there were the maestros of the game even then; the Manchester City hero Frank Swift – by a sad irony he actually died with Manchester United players at Munich in his second career as journalist. Frank could apparently pick a football up by spanning his hand around its circumference, and he was said to have a hand span of just slightly under a foot. Raich Carter suggested that when Frank was in goal, it might've been easier to get the ball into a matchbox – and he should know; a great centre-forward, he played for Sunderland, Derby and Hull City, as well as England. Frank Swift was always willing to give advice to young goalkeepers and would often reflect with his own hand-drawn diagrams where he considered how a goal might've been saved.

Frank Swift's successor at Manchester City was a German lad called Bert Trautmann, who Gordon said was a direct influence on his game. Bert was a specialist in stopping shots, but he was also as good as any other in the air. He was not the penalty-taker's best friend, as he is reputed to have saved about 60 per cent of them. Strikers were advised not to look up as Bert could read where they were going to place their shot – it may have been best to shoot and hope for the best. He was also a great thrower of the ball to start the counter-attack, but one of his greatest attributes was that he was fearless: he dived at strikers' feet and had many injuries as a consequence, including a broken neck after which he played on. Bert lived to the ripe old age of eighty-nine! Lev Yashin, the Russian goalkeeping legend, said Bert was a world-class goalkeeper, but with transport a little less reliable and available than it is today, playing in the English First Division back then made an international career impossible. Bert Williams was an inspiration to Gordon, and he played for Wolverhampton Wanderers over 400 times, winning a League title and the FA Cup. Bert was capped by England, playing his part in the 1950 World Cup finals.

Blackpool's goalkeeper, George Farm, was an early pioneer of the idea that a sound defence was one organised by the goalkeeper. This was not a widespread practice at the time, but it was enough to make Gordon take note.

Of course it does rely on a good defence, but still the odd thing can get through. The Newcastle United and Manchester City (traditional) centre-forward, Wyn Davies, could head a ball as hard as any, but one time Gordon anticipated what Wyn was going to do and was able to pull off one of his own favourite saves. He relates in his autobiography how George Best dribbled the ball past the Stoke City defenders before wrong-footing the goalkeeper (himself), who finished up on his 'arse'. On the subject of Manchester United, Bobby Charlton made Gordon's hands tingle from his youth days at Chesterfield until his later days with Stoke City.

Leaving the save against Pelé a moment, because God knows how many million saw that at the time and now draw it up on the internet frequently, it is a Geoff Hurst attempt that can also demonstrate how a goalkeeper can read a striker's intentions. In the semi-final of the Football League Cup in the 1971/72 season, West Ham's Harry Redknapp was almost around Gordon when he was felled. Penalty! So up came Geoff to take the spot-kick. But in the mind of Gordon, Geoff's behaviour was the same as earlier in the tie when he'd scored from a penalty. So when Geoff made his run and Gordon waited for the thud of boot on leather, he had a fraction of a second to dive to his right, where the ball followed the exact same path as the earlier one. A spectacular save put Stoke City into their first Wembley Cup final. So it is plain the role of the goalkeeping coach is now essential to any team, as is reflecting on goals conceded – learn from goalkeepers and learn from outfield players. When one considers all of one's lifetimes mistakes and learns from them, it is called experience. Albert Camus, who was himself a good goalkeeper, said, 'You cannot create experience. You must undergo it.'

3

The Road to Chesterfield

As a lad, Gordon was not particularly gifted academically, and his life looked as though it would be mainly labouring jobs that he'd take up. With the coal merchants, he'd been too exhausted to even think about football. But it's said that no experience is ever wasted, so when he moved on to his bricklaying apprenticeship and his early jobs were in hod carrying, he was all set to consolidate the strength he had built up in the coal business. As hod carrying meant climbing ladders loaded up, then his leg muscles would develop and, just as importantly, his sense of balance would be enhanced.

His experiences in the Sheffield Schoolboys' team had not attracted much interest, but his easy-going nature meant he was satisfied with his general lot in life. At weekends he'd sometimes potter along to local amateur sides, and one Saturday he was ready to watch the local works team, Millspaugh, who had a rather strange goalkeeper who had a habit of not turning up for their games. The trainer didn't seem particularly perturbed, however, as he'd seen a young lad on the touchline that he recognised as a goalkeeper – and a good one too. He'd seen Gordon play for the Sheffield Schoolboys side, so their temporary goalkeeping vacancy was a chance for Gordon to have a better afternoon – once he had dashed home to collect his boots. He didn't have any shorts but the trainer managed to find a goalkeeper's shirt, so he tucked his trousers into his socks and was all set. Gordon referred to this as 'open-aged' football because, although he was only fifteen, most of the other players were in their twenties. Things went fairly well on his debut match and the result was a 2-2 draw. The team manager was impressed and, with the regular goalkeeper being absent, he invited Gordon back to play again for them. In fact, he played for Millspaugh for the majority of the rest of the season, and for a lad easily pleased, Gordon was happy with the team.

More than one person saw his potential though, and the following year he was asked to sign for the much higher-grade football team of Rawmarsh

Welfare, who played in the Yorkshire League. A lot of local amateur football had fallen by the wayside during the First World War, and the Yorkshire League was reformed in 1920, with semi-professional and amateur local football teams. Some League clubs entered their reserves and third teams, and the League survived until the 1980s. It was a competitive League and there were only six seasons when a title wasn't competed for, which was unsurprisingly during and immediately after the Second World War. After the war, Bradford Park Avenue reserves won the title. This attracted other clubs, but the Bradford team, together with Selby Town, enjoyed the most success. Within a few years, there were two divisions; in 1961, a third was added but didn't last. In the Second Division, Stocksbridge Works had become a strong side in the 1950s. They were soon in the top flight and became champions – and retained it for the following four seasons.

So with highflyers around like Stocksbridge Works, it proved the ideal opportunity and when the chance presented itself, Gordon thought he was ready. So did others, but in his debut match for Rawmarsh Welfare – an away game at the mighty Stocksbridge Works – they were well beaten 12-2. Next game, which was a home fixture, the side were beaten 3-1. Following this, Gordon's tenure in the Rawmarsh goal came to an abrupt end. That's a bit sad really because a goalkeeper is the last line of defence, and defending should start with the outfield players – a good goalkeeper is said to be worth a good few goals in a season, but with a good back line one expects them to be worth a few more.

The following Saturday, Gordon was at Millspaugh's patch, and lo and behold their goalkeeper hadn't turned up. Gordon was later to say that with the twice-weekly training sessions with Millspaugh, and the weekend match, he would have been quite content with life as it was. The most important thing was that football was back in his life as part of the regular routine, and he said he was now taking his football much more seriously.

Towards the end of the season, this would be in the spring of 1953, Gordon was still doing well with Millspaugh and by now had stopped taking too much notice of who was watching the games – he knew that a goalkeeper's concentration should be on the game! After one particular match, he was approached by a man who'd been watching the game. Arthur Sutherland had made the journey up from Chesterfield, about 9 miles or so, to watch the game, and said he was willing to give Gordon a trial at Chesterfield, who played their senior club games in the old Third Division (North). Gordon was headed for their youth team, and if he was good enough, then the next season would give him perhaps more opportunity.

So with his sights still only set a level or two higher, Gordon braved the late March winds and rain to arrive at Chesterfield's Saltergate ground for his first training session. Strangely, he was set to work on a punching bag. Part of a goalkeeper's skill is to know when to punch the ball clear, which only staved off the attack, and when he might catch a ball, effectively ending the attack and starting a counter-attack. Primitive though it was, the benefits were good and far-reaching. No exercise or training time is ever wasted and, if focused, the skill or discipline is easily transferred to the football field; Gordon said he always felt confident and able when punching a ball clear.

The youth team at Chesterfield played in the Northern Intermediate League, and in the mid-1950s the up-and-coming players would hope to progress to the more senior sides, initially the reserves. Gordon was quite firmly footed on the bottom rung of the ladder and the only way was up – most of the time!

The town of Chesterfield in Derbyshire lies some 140-odd miles north of London. Its main claim to fame is the strange shape of the spire on one of its town centre churches, and its football club now carry the nickname of The Spireites.

The story behind the unique spire on the church of St Mary and All Saints has its own twists! It was said that a blacksmith who had just re-shod the devil didn't do a good job, and in his despair, the devil leapt over the spire and left his mark, though there are variations to this theme. Another claim is that a virgin got married in the church and the spire will straighten up when another virgin goes up the aisle! However, it's more likely the use of unseasoned timber or the lack of skilled tradesmen just after the Great Plague was a factor. There is apparently little mention of the deformities of the spire until the original wooden roof was replaced by heavy slates and lead, so one might be inclined to look at its construction. Chesterfield's spire is not unique; St Peters in Barnstaple, Devon, and a church in Cleobury Mortimer, Shropshire, also have spires that are out of the ordinary, but not half as deformed. There are also dozens of examples in France.

Chesterfield is a market town, which received its Royal Charter in 1204, and still has a huge market. Mining was a staple of the area for many years, and there were a number of local collieries, though little evidence remains of the industry now. The coalfield was discovered during tunnelling when the railway expansion saw the building of the Leeds to Derby line, which was overseen by George Stevenson himself.

The first football club can be traced back to the third part of the nineteenth century, but its history was not one of high-flyers; they did, however, have some success in cup tournaments around their local area. The club turned professional near the end of the century, and entered the FA Cup in 1892. During the First World War, there was something of a scandal and the FA suspended the club due to payment irregularities. But the folk of Chesterfield loved their football so the local council started a football club, which was the origin of the current one.

The FA suggested the club sever its ties with the council, which it did and became Chesterfield FC in 1921. They joined the then Third Division (North) and soon after, in 1926, the man who became Gordon's first manager joined the club as manager! Edward (Ted) Davison had enjoyed a long playing career as a goalkeeper for Sheffield Wednesday before entering management as player-manager at Mansfield Town – who were then a non-League side. He was to return to Sheffield for another prolonged stint, but now as manager at Sheffield United. Ted wasn't a tall, gangly man, so his success as a goalkeeper had been down to his reading of the game and his quick reflexes. In fact, during his career he would save just under a third of the penalties he had to deal with! As a manager he wanted to keep the footballing side separate from the admin side of the job, though he was quite a methodical record keeper. He also had a respect for experienced players, and in his fourth season with Mansfield they had some success in gaining promotion to the Second Division.

Ted also knew the importance of a youth policy, and established a good scouting network. Mansfield is only a short distance from Chesterfield and the club became aware of Ted's tenacity. After his first season at Mansfield, he gave up the playing side because of injury and started to consolidate his management style. This impressed Chesterfield so much that when the job of manager became vacant they went head-hunting; offering £6 a week, they got the man they wanted.

In those days, managers stayed with clubs for a number of seasons. The Sheffield United boss, John Nicholson – who was actually in charge for over thirty years – had died in early 1932, and so Ted was approached to take over the team; he stayed with Sheffield United for twenty years.

The role of the manager had changed in the first fifty years or so of the League's existence, and in some cases the role had been labelled as secretary. The post was created at Sheffield United when the club became a limited company in 1899. There was a trainer and the team was selected by a panel, but it was the 'secretary' who looked after the players each day.

After John Nicholson's death and Ted Davison's twenty years at the club, they were seemingly stuck mid-table in the Second Division and were having some difficulty bouncing back to the First Division from which they were relegated in 1949. It was at this time that Ted reassessed his future.

He made the trek back to Chesterfield, and although he signed a couple of experienced players, the club were in financial difficulties, as most of the country was with post-war austerity, and he only had fourteen full professionals on the staff. But Ted had a good youth policy and Chesterfield reached the FA Youth Cup final in 1956, with Gordon in goal. They were to face cup-holders Manchester United, who'd beaten West Bromwich Albion 7-1 the previous season. For the first time, Gordon faced future world-class players: Bobby Charlton, Wilf McGuinness, and others of the Busby Babes. For the first leg at Old Trafford, the crowd was a staggering 32,000. Against such a distinguished team, the juniors still managed to only lose by a single goal at 3-2. The second leg at the Recreation Ground, known as Saltergate (after the road the ground was in), finished up with one goal apiece, so Manchester United won on aggregate 4-3, and with a 14,000 crowd (the average for the first team was 9,000) the youngsters had done well. It was Manchester United's fourth FA Youth Cup final in succession.

It is true to say that, as well as the attributes of skill, vision, agility and strength, a goalkeeper needs a great deal of courage – not to mention a keen anticipation of what the striker approaching his goal is going to do. So injuries are an occupational hazard. Gordon was out injured for a few weeks after he dived at the feet of a forward to save 'a certain goal' and fractured his elbow, and the fragments had to be screwed together. By now, Gordon was fluctuating between the youth team and the reserves, before finding himself mainly as the reserve-team goalkeeper. But he was still only a part-time professional, training with the club two nights a week and then arriving at the ground on the Saturday to see what was happening. It wasn't easy as he had to travel to the ground by bus, but it was an exciting period in his life.

He'd continued to work as a bricklayer's apprentice, but all of that changed when he went off to do his National Service. In Germany, as a dispatch rider for the Royal Signals, he met Ursula, his future wife, and when he returned to Saltergate in Chesterfield he was ready to dedicate himself to professional football. When he finished his National Service, Chesterfield were ready to take Gordon on as a full-time professional.

In fact, they were more than ready because, through his performances with his regiment's own team, word had filtered back that this man had a lot of potential. Chesterfield didn't want to lose him. Gordon described it as an 'escape' from bricklaying, and with a new wife and in the sport he loved, he was a happy man. They settled in the village of Treeton, just outside of Chesterfield, and lived in a modest terraced house with a few borrowed bits of parental furniture and a mortgage of £1,100 – at Leicester the club owned houses so he could rent one of those initially.

Throughout his time in the youth team and reserves, Gordon had waited patiently to progress. The first-team goalkeeper was Ron Powell, a veteran who would notch up well over 400 games before a road accident forced his retirement from the game – one hopes this wasn't an omen.

In the meantime, Gordon and Ursula (Mrs Banks) were very happy, and their family grew in July 1958 when son Robert was born. Life for the hands of the Chesterfield goalkeeper tended to revolve around his son, nappies and helping around the house – but this was a changing trend. In his autobiography, Gordon describes how Ursula took naturally to motherhood.

But on the field, pressure was mounting on Ron Powell as Gordon was keen to get on. Ron may have been a veteran, but he was still the right side of thirty for a goalkeeper, so competition was intense. How long would England's future greatest be an understudy? Ted Davison, on the other hand, was now the wrong side of seventy, and in May of 1958 he decided to call it a day and retired to Sheffield. Retirement isn't exactly accurate though, as he continued to do a bit of scouting.

In came the new Chesterfield manager, Dugald 'Duggie' Livingstone. He was a much-travelled Scot who'd played both at right- and left-back for Celtic, Everton and Plymouth Argyle, before he returned to Scotland to play for Aberdeen. Duggie finished his playing days with Tranmere Rovers. He was later to be Ted Davison's assistant manager at Sheffield United, and when he broke into senior management, he took Newcastle United to the FA Cup final and the Belgian national team to the World Cup finals. He also spent a couple of seasons managing the Republic of Ireland national team.

At Newcastle, things were not apparently to his liking and it was the board that had the final say in team selection. This was dying out, but even with Newcastle United winning the FA Cup in 1955, Duggie still wasn't happy about board team selection. So he went south to London to manage Fulham in 1956 for a couple of seasons, before finishing up at Chesterfield in 1958. He was to stay until 1959.

Gordon's stint with the first team at Chesterfield is worth a close look. For the 1958/59 season, the old Third Division South and North were amalgamated and became the Third and Fourth Divisions. Chesterfield's opponents for Gordon's first match were Colchester United from the old Third Division south, so a completely unknown quantity.

A total attendance of 7,140 was recorded at the Recreation Ground – Saltergate – for the game on Saturday 29 November 1958. Playing conditions were described as atrocious, with a fog covering proceedings, and conditions continued to deteriorate. But the debut goalkeeper for Chesterfield – referred to as the Blues in their local press rather than The Spirites – was going to show all 7,140 or, at any rate those who could see the Chesterfield goal, just how good he was.

Arthur Bottom also made his debut for the Blues in that match, another Sheffield-born player, though more experienced in his role. Arthur came from Newcastle United, whom he had helped avoid relegation, but he'd made his name as a prolific goalscorer at York City. Now, at twenty-eight, he was head of Chesterfield's attack at centre-forward.

After only ten minutes, Colchester were making their mark; a 'pinpoint' centre from the Colchester winger Russell Blake was headed past Gordon by Peter Wright. Peter played for Colchester United more than 450 times, and was one of their star players – scoring after ten minutes from a pinpoint cross with a header past Gordon Banks was something even Pelé didn't achieve. Peter Wright had attracted attention from several of the 'bigger' clubs, but remained with Colchester. He was hailed as an all-time great by the club and its supporters.

But the Blues were not going to let Colchester have it all their own way. Wing-half Maurice Galley equalised, and then a minute later inside-right Bryan Frear put them ahead with the score at half-time Chesterfield two, Colchester one.

The second half got underway with the Blues hoping to hold on to their lead and give Gordon a winning debut. But the afternoon really belonged to the Colchester star. On seventy-five minutes, Peter Wright sent over a long cross and Gordon was stranded and unsighted – the ball hit the far post and went in. The result was a 2-2 draw and the local press reported, 'Banks ... could not be blamed for Colchester's goals, and he brought off some excellent saves.'

And then, the FA Cup. Gordon was to play in two FA Cup finals, but not with Chesterfield. This one was a second-round cup tie away to Carlisle United; the result giving the young Chesterfield goalkeeper another milestone in his career, a first clean sheet, and yet another milestone when he saved his first penalty. The match was reported to have displayed the 'brilliance ... of the Chesterfield defence ... Banks was again in fine form'. The match finished as a goalless draw, so a replay was to take place – this happened at Saltergate four days later on Wednesday 10 December, with Chesterfield winning by the only goal. Bryan Frear scored in the seventy-first minute, and so the young goalkeeper kept a clean sheet yet again.

Three days later, Chesterfield were hosts in a League match to Norwich City, and another fine display was accredited to Gordon. The match finished at one goal apiece. Gwyn Lewis scored for Chesterfield, but the press were to suggest Chesterfield were a little weak in attack. Nevertheless, the defence were in fine fettle and it was reported that Arsenal scouts were watching Gordon. Gerry Sears actually cleared the ball with his hand at one stage. Norwich centre-forward Terry Allcock, who equalised in the final few minutes, had said it was over the line, Gerry admitted it was but he had actually cleared the ball with his hand. He said later, 'I was amazed to get away with it.'

Five days before Christmas of 1958, the Blues travelled up to Yorkshire where Halifax Town beat them 3-2 and Gordon's skill at penalty saving was tested in the last minute following a controversial refereeing decision.

Halifax's centre-forward, Alan Blackburn, and Gordon both went for a loose ball and Gordon seemed to get there first, but the Halifax man went sprawling. Conway Smith converted the spot-kick to complete the tally started earlier by Peter Tilley and Alan Blackburn – Arthur Bottom and Dave Blakey scored for Chesterfield.

The Chesterfield first team trained on that Christmas Day as they had two fixtures over the holiday, against Wrexham at Saltergate on Boxing Day, and away to the same team on 27 December. At first glance, the results seemed bizarre. At home they drew one goal apiece – Don Weston scored for Wrexham and Bryan Frear for the hosts – but away at Wrexham the following day, they won 4-3. The Boxing Day fixture was described as a lacklustre game and the conditions were poor. For the return match, Duggie Livingstone reshuffled the team a bit and it seemed to have the desired effect. But defence is as important as the strike force, and three goals conceded needed some thought – but whoever was doing the thinking didn't think Gordon should lose his place in the team. On New Year's Day 1959, Chesterfield beat Hull City 2-1 in front of a huge crowd of 10,374 – Gwyn Lewis and Keith Havenhand scoring for the Blues and Bill Bradbury answering for the visitors.

The forward line (in those days it was of two wingers, two inside-forwards and a centre-forward) were beginning to produce a series of results. On 3 January 1959, Chesterfield hosted Newport County at home. But despite the Chesterfield press praising Newport goalkeeper Len Weare – who would make 525 appearances by the time he retired from football in 1970 – the Blues took the two points that Saturday. The final result was a comfortable three goals – Gwyn Lewis in each half and Bryan Frear – to one win and 'Banks again showed how good he is'.

The population also made the news at the time when they were thanked for the help they had given in the Crooked Spire Fund; they raised over £3,000.

On 10 January, the team travelled to Colchester for a third-round FA Cup tie. They had drawn 2-2 earlier in the season on Gordon's debut. But on this day the Essex side went ahead when Gordon parried a shot but didn't hold it, and striker John Evans was there to tap the loose ball into the net. But control was difficult on the frozen pitch. After the half-time hot cup of tea, Chesterfield fell further behind after fifty-three minutes when a poor back pass by centre-half Dave Blakey was intercepted by Neil Langman and Colchester United went two up. 'Big' David Blakey was a one-club man. Born in Newburn, not far from Newcastle, in August 1929, he served the Blues loyally after joining from East Chevington Juniors local youth side, He made over 600 appearances over nineteen years and scored twenty goals – but one wonders just how many this long-serving player helped prevent. He is singled out in Gordon's autobiography, though he praises all his Chesterfield teammates, as being helpful in his gaining the confidence to start directing his defence to what he felt he needed.

Colchester player John Evans is also worth pausing for. He'd played for Liverpool, where in September 1954 he scored all five goals in their defeat of Bristol Rovers. Ian Rush and Robbie Fowler were to later join this elite group. In January 1904, Andy McGuigan made history as the first Liverpool player to score five goals in a single match when Stoke City visited Anfield and were defeated 7-0. But things were a bit uneven in that match; the Stoke players were reportedly suffering from food poisoning and would leave the pitch at intervals to vomit or whatever – at one time Stoke were down to seven men! It was a fish supper that was to blame, but I couldn't discover whether the goalkeeper was a victim, nor could I find any details of the chef – I wanted to know if he had later worked in Mexico!

Meanwhile, back in the first season of Gordon at Chesterfield, things hit a bit of a high point when they went to Southend in mid-January 1959 and had a resounding 5-2 victory. But the press didn't see it as a high point, merely commenting the side were the 'old unpredictable'. Bryan Frear, a great servant to Chesterfield, scored a hat-trick; he was to play 281 games for the Blues over six seasons, scoring a total of eighty-four goals before he moved on to Halifax Town. Barry Hutchinson scored the other Chesterfield goals.

Reading were promotion hopefuls in the 1958/59 season, but when Chesterfield visited on 24 January they were anything but sparkling. The visitors won 2-1, with Keith Havenhand and Arthur Bottom both getting on the scoresheet.

On 31 January, Chesterfield made the short trip to Notts County's Meadow Lane ground. Notts County are one of the oldest football teams in the country, and in 1903 supplied a set of their shirts to Juventus, who thereafter adopted the black-and-white stripes. The Blues were said to 'lack bite' that afternoon and finished up conceding three goals to their one scored – Andy McCabe did the honours. It was said that Gordon had an 'off day' that day, and he was criticised by the press who suggested two of the goals could have been saved.

The turnaround came the following week when they cruised to a 3-1 win over another local team, Mansfield Town. It was said that the performance against Notts County was a mystery, but the attraction of football is sometimes the odd hiccup in a side's performance, and if at Notts County Gordon did make a couple of errors and the forward line 'lacked bite' that doesn't sound all that mysterious. Against Mansfield, Gordon didn't touch the ball for the first ten minutes; though he did dig the ball out of the net when Mansfield scored their goal. It was just over twenty minutes into the second half when Barry Hutchinson, who Gordon said was a particularly good friend at Chesterfield, made a poor back pass, which Barrie Thomas intercepted and scored.

On 14 February, they made the trip to the West Country to take on Swindon Town at the County Ground. Swindon were reportedly 'poor opposition' but still managed to score through Maurice Owen. Bryan Frear and Arthur Bottom ensured the points went back to Saltergate. A controversial penalty took the points away from Saltergate on their next home tie against Brentford, and the disputed penalty that stole the show – left-back Gerry Sears maintained his handball was accidental; George Francis scored from the penalty spot and Jim Towers added a second after the interval. Bryan Frear scored for Chesterfield and then it went back to Gerry Sears for a second. Gerry was a stalwart campaigner for the Blues, making 412 appearances over sixteen seasons at the club. He came up from the youth team, making his first-team debut in 1952, after his 412th appearance he retired completely from football.

But against Brentford that day, Gerry's handball apart, the attack was said to be 'slow'. Uncharacteristically, Gordon didn't have a good match, and the press reported that he didn't seem too confident – his handling brought some 'gasps' from the supporters. Gasps were to become a regular feature of Gordon's game, but usually for quite different reasons. But the trade of goalkeeping in those days developed without dedicated coaches, so it was very much a 'learn on the job' challenge for them.

On the last day of February, Queens Park Rangers (QPR) came to Saltergate and took the points back to Shepherd's Bush; 'A Weak Display' was the headline. Some criticism was levelled at Gordon: 'This was just not Banks' day and several times during the game he looked unsafe.' This seems to me to be a bit of an all-embracing statement, and through the subsequent report it looked as though he was at fault for the first goal, for the second he was unsighted and for the third he had to come off his line before Clive Clark chipped the ball over him – players who chipped the ball over Gordon became fewer and further between, and one outstanding save against Scotland later in his career is something I want to describe later. Right-back Gerry Clarke scored the first Chesterfield goal, Arthur Bottom added in the second half, but the final score was Chesterfield two, QPR three.

The events of the matches and the reporting didn't always marry up, and criticism was brutal at times: 'this sort of insipid football' and 'attack which was practically clueless'.

However, the Blues travelled up to Rochdale and secured a point with a goalless draw, Gordon's first clean sheet for a while, though as I have pointed out there are defenders, so this doesn't reflect on the goalkeeper as much as people would like to suggest. The match was notable for long-range shots: 'Everyone except Banks tried one.' But things were looking up and 'it was good to see Banks more like his old self'; a superb diving save just before the end was noted.

As March came, a trip to Doncaster only attracted 4,600-odd supporters and it was supposedly a dull affair, but with the Chesterfield goalkeeper saving a penalty this doesn't quite fit. He pushed it onto the bar but the ball was then hooked over the line courtesy of wing-half Tommy Cavanagh. Centre-forward Jim Fletcher scored the winner in the second half, and Keith Havenhand had scored for Chesterfield in the first half.

A visit to Plymouth Argyle on 21 March saw the home team ahead through Reg Jenkins. Wilf Carter drove a fierce shot that Gordon was unable to hold and Reg was there to pick up the rebound. It was Wilf Carter himself who scored the second; both goals came in the first half. A crowd of over 17,000 saw this match!

But Gordon's confidence grew with his skill. Bury visited Saltergate and three goals later Chesterfield were easy winners, with Gordon having long periods of inactivity. But Bury got their revenge three days later with a 1-0 win, and in between the two Bury fixtures the Blues were beaten by Tranmere Rovers 3-2 – Gordon was in bed with flu for these two fixtures. He was back for their 1-0 win at home to Bournemouth, with James Maddison scoring in the first half. This game was marred in one sense by a collision that resulted in two players leaving the pitch for hospital; the Bournemouth goalkeeper, Tommy Godwin, collided with outside-right Andy McCabe. Tommy had rib injuries and Andy had broken his leg. However, the two teams of ten men played some good football and a fierce shot from 'Dickie' Dowsett for Bournemouth brought about a superb save from Gordon. For Andy McCabe, it was the end of his footballing career and his health was a constant worry until his death in 1963 at the age of twenty-eight.

On the heels of the Bournemouth victory was another single-goal win over Stockport County, again at home with Gwyn Lewis getting the winner in the second half. A trip to Colchester on 18 April saw them lose by a single goal, but the following Saturday they completed the double over Reading with a one goal to nil win at Saltergate in driving rain in their penultimate game of the campaign. Centre-forward Keith Havenhand, who'd been injured early in the game, scored the winner shortly after the interval. The rain made playing conditions hazardous, and defensive errors were almost inevitable. Dave Blakey made a perilous back pass from which Reading nearly equalised. Gordon got a hand to the shot, but it still headed towards the goal – left-back Ivor Seemley cleared off the line.

The last appearance for Chesterfield came on the last Saturday of the season in a 2-1 defeat at Norwich City; Gwyn Lewis got the goal. It was reported Gordon played well in the game, and it seems the bigger clubs already had an eye on his performance. His inclusion in the team was now likely to mean he would be the first-choice goalkeeper, although Ron Powell managed to knock up his 300th appearance in the 1958/59 season, and played on for another five or six seasons.

So the future England anchor made twenty-three League and three FA Cup appearances for Chesterfield FC. I don't think that the statistics of goals conceded would give anything like an accurate description of Gordon's performance for the club, but for anyone interested, during that time the team conceded thirty-four goals and scored forty. At least two of the goals were from disputed penalties, and a number were because of defensive rather than goalkeeping errors. Gordon's first part-season in the Football League saw him keep seven clean sheets and veteran goalkeeper Ron Powell in the reserves, only coming back when a dose of flu put Gordon out of the line-up. I mentioned the record of Dave Blakey earlier, but Ron Powell's final tally was also impressive; he is second in the list of appearances at Chesterfield, making a total of 471 starts. On the eve of his 300th appearance he was sidelined, though in his autobiography Gordon said Ron was 'all right' about it. He must have recognised Gordon's worth, and perhaps even wondered how long it would be before the big clubs came looking. He didn't have to wonder for long.

It was in May 1959 that the *Derbyshire Times* and the *Chesterfield Herald* reported Gordon had been transferred to Leicester City. This apparently shocked and angered some supporters, as the last line of defence had turned out to be a player of outstanding calibre.

There was talk of the club selling him so they could pay their rates, when most would have hoped the money would have been used for some team-building venture. The reporter went on to say, 'There are ample mediocre players ... could be dispensed with without being missed, but only disaster can follow if any of the few remaining competent players are allowed to go.' The chairman, Harold Shentall, said the club was losing money every week despite the infusion of funds from Chesterfield's Sportsmen's Association, and the Supporters' Club also gave some assistance. The board were perhaps avoiding the real issues, and some suggestion was made that they should not expect the public to pay expenses they incurred, so one wonders where some of the money was going. With a maximum wage and good gates the equation didn't seem to make sense.

The argument the press were getting around to was that there was a need for a more diverse make-up in the board of directors at the club, therefore giving some accountability as to where the money went and why such a good young player was sold. With the fact that the supporters had to all intents and purposes raised the money for the purchase of Arthur Bottom, there was some suggestion the integrity of the board wasn't all it should have been.

Duggie Livingstone was not blamed for what had happened, though it seemed he felt Gordon's potential was great and a First Division club was the place for him, but the press thought there might be as many people watching as playing the next season!

Chesterfield finished in sixteenth position in the Third Division in its first season. From forty-six games played they won seventeen, lost nineteen and drew ten; they scored sixty-seven goals and conceded sixty-four.

4

Leicester City
To Begin With...

Gordon hadn't given a lot of thought to his future and his plans were simple, keep out as many goals as possible for Chesterfield, polish up his art – and science – and enjoy his home life. Robert was getting on for two years old, so as the 1950s came to an end, life was looking good.

Chesterfield manager Duggie Livingstone called Gordon into his office one day, and with him was what Gordon described as 'a dapper man with wavy black hair'. It was Matt Gillies, manager of Leicester City, and the offer of £7,000 had been made for his signature. Duggie was a good man and explained why he wanted Gordon to stay at Saltergate, but he also explained that the move would benefit Gordon's career immensely.

Matt Gillies had been at Leicester for many years, as player, coach and, from November 1958, a club manager. To get one of the most outstanding talents in goalkeeping for such a moderate fee was a coup, but Matt was a clever man at spotting potential in youngsters. He had a fifteen-year-old called Peter Shilton waiting in the wings!

Leicester have had football on their doorstep since the 1880s, and had a League side called Leicester Fosse (Leicester is on the Roman road, Fosse Way) who were playing at a ground in Filbert Street from the early 1890s. After the First World War there were some financial difficulties and the club broke up, but it reformed as Leicester City Football Club in 1921. They did tend to enjoy mixed fortunes though, moving up to the First Division and down to the second a few times, but in 1957 they moved up to the top flight and remained there until 1969. They were FA Cup finalists on three occasions during those years, though on each occasion were runners-up – I will discuss the two finals in which Gordon played in 1961 and 1963 later. In 1969, a Neil Young goal for Manchester City took the trophy back to Maine Road. Leicester also competed in two Football League Cup finals in the early 1960s – they were victorious over Stoke City but were beaten by Chelsea, again something to consider. In those days, the Football League Cup was new and the final was over two legs: at home and away. There was also European football and Tottenham Hotspur, as League champions, competed in the European Cup, while Leicester, as runners-up in the FA Cup, qualified for the European Cup Winners' Cup. In the 1962/63 season they finished fourth in the League; at one time that season they were top of the League.

There were a number of goalkeepers at Leicester when Gordon joined them, but in a couple of pre-season friendlies he gave a good account of himself and was pleasantly surprised to find he was selected to play in the reserves on the first Saturday of the 1959/60 season, at home to Southend United. The reserve team was part of the Football Combination, of which they had been champions the previous season. The match against Southend reserves finished as a goalless draw, but it was the start of a fairly good run for Gordon in the reserves, only conceding four goals in four games; his best performance he felt was in a 2-0 defeat at home by Chelsea reserves.

The first-choice goalkeeper was Dave MacLaren, who had come to Leicester from Dundee in 1957, and left for Plymouth Argyle in 1960, where he enjoyed a good few seasons before coming back up to the Midlands with Wolverhampton Wanderers. After playing he was briefly a manager.

Gordon wasn't the only newcomer that season; other debutants were striker Albert Cheesebrough (his daughter became a world-class gymnast) and half-back Frank McLintock – later an international and captain of the all-conquering Arsenal in the early 1970s.

Dave MacLaren had injured a finger, so on Wednesday 9 September 1960 Gordon made his First Division debut for Leicester City. The visitors to Filbert Street were Blackpool, though Stanley Matthews didn't play that night. But another of Gordon's great heroes, goalkeeper George Farm, did. And who would deny Gordon a long moment of pride from the press write-up: 'Gordon Banks, 21-year-old husky Sheffielder, making a dependable-looking debut for the City, outshone international George Farm', and the match report went on to say 'Banks began countless moves'. One notable thing about the way Gordon played was his preference to throw the ball out to start a counter-attack through the flanks, rather than the big boot upfield, which often meant the ball could fall into the opposition's possession – a throw out would more accurately target a player, and possession for the start of the counter-attack was more likely. In watching a good few of his games, his sense of urgency in getting the ball out is evident. The result of the Blackpool match was a goal each, which was thought a fair result, though half a minute from the end, Blackpool's right-half Jim Kelly hit the post with 'a stunner'. Ken Leek, Leicester's dependable inside-forward, had scored in the sixty-second minute. He was there to pick up on a shot that George Farm could only parry, and so slotted the ball into goal. Jackie Mudie equalised for Blackpool; 'with cool poise' he placed the ball past Gordon, who was quickly out to narrow the angle.

But it could have gone either way as the Jim Kelly final-minute drive showed; though Leicester's outside-left Gordon Wills also sent a volley just wide earlier in the match. The new man in goal had done well and was said to have made some fine saves, notably one from Ray Charnley, which was described as a 'great'. Overall Leicester had tended to dawdle and had wanted too much time with the ball, and you didn't get that with the 'mighty Blackpool' – Gordon's description – in those days.

On 12 September they were at home to Newcastle United, and according to one observer they 'failed in temperament, technique and tactics'. Jackie Bell scored twice for Newcastle, but Albert Cheesebrough missed a penalty. Confidence wasn't high and not even Gordon attracted a good word; in fact, the particular commentator thought that his failure to stop the two long shots by Jackie Bell, from which the goals resulted, was because he was unsighted.

Dave MacLaren was to return to the first team, but this didn't return Leicester to winning ways; in the next five games poor old Dave was spending far too much time in his own net retrieving the ball for the next kick-off! So Gordon returned to the first team for a trip to Maine Road and a 3-2 defeat by Manchester City.

Thus far in the 1959/60 season Leicester City had only had one win, which was against Birmingham City, but even then it was a 4-3 scoreline. The defence needed some attention, and Gordon's recall to the first team didn't lead to overnight success. In the next three matches they conceded eleven goals, though the season did start to move a little more smoothly and, on 7 November, they beat Sheffield Wednesday 2-0 – a victory, but as importantly, a clean sheet. The game before this is worth looking at though because Leicester City conceded six goals and then suddenly got a clean sheet. So something went horribly wrong, but just as quickly, things resolved themselves and the season turned around.

A crowd of 22,589 braved the Merseyside drizzle to see Leicester annihilated on Saturday 31 October 1959. It was called a 'duel of the First Division lowly' by the acerbic *Leicester Evening Mail* reporter.

The first half was punctuated by an Everton penalty, which Bobby Collins converted, and a Leicester City penalty, which Albert Cheesebrough didn't. Everton striker Alan Shackleton hit the woodwork twice so was unlucky. At the other end the target was more elusive, Ken Leek missed by a mile and a Ken Keyworth shot was intercepted.

Back on the attack, Everton's Jimmy Harris centred for Bobby Collins, but the ball bounced off a defender. Ken Keyworth went close for Leicester when he followed up on Albert Cheesebrough's strike, and the Leicester defence were getting on top of things with John Newman and Joe Baillie. The fine drizzle didn't help, with passes frequently going astray. Gordon punched out a corner and he cut out a Jimmy Harris cross. Leicester mounted an attack that saw Ken Keyworth picking up on Len Chalmers' chip and a goal looked inevitable, but didn't materialise. An own goal almost gave Everton the advantage when John Newman narrowly missed his own crossbar – heading over! Shortly after, he collided with Mr Aston, the referee.

Len Chalmers was adjudged to have elbowed Alan Shackleton. Penalty! Bobby Collins hit it home. Leicester were down but not out, and shortly after Ken Keyworth saw his effort cleared off the line by Alex Parker. The counter-attack saw Gordon almost pulling the ball from Bobby Collins' head. Then Ken Keyworth went close with a diving header. Just before half-time, Ken Leek's header was fisted off the line by full-back Alex Parker, the penalty wasn't converted though.

Half-time: Everton 1, Leicester 0.

The drizzle persisted, the floodlights were on. Everton were far more adventurous with the ball, moving from wing to wing, but the Leicester defence looked safe. In the fifty-first minute Jimmy Harris centred and Bobby Laverick tried to hammer the ball in, but it hit inside-forward Eddie Thomas and went in anyway. At 2-0, Leicester were in trouble. Albert Cheesebrough led them towards the Everton goal, but on the slippery pitch lost his footing when a goal looked likely.

Bobby Collins looked dangerous and his shot across goal bounced into the path of Alan Shackleton to make the score 3-0. It was nearly four when Collins hit a hard strike, but Gordon was more than equal and flicked the ball over the bar. Left-half Brian Harris put Everton four up with a 25-yard drive, and Alex Parker scored number five from just outside the 18-yard box. Consolation came just over ten minutes from time when Tommy McDonald headed home an Albert Cheesebrough cross.

But Everton were not finished yet, and a cross from the left wing was headed in by Eddie Thomas. So things crumbled in the second half – could the Leicester lads come up with a solution? They could and they did; the final score Everton 6, Leicester City 1.

The referee was Kenneth Aston of Ilford, who was once assisted by armed police to keep order in a 1962 Chilean World Cup game. Later, just after the infamous Argentinian Antonio Rattín incident in the 1966 World Cup, he got the inspiration for the yellow card for caution or red for dismissal: Mr Rattín's claim to not understand, if that was what it was, would soon be a thing of the past.

Meanwhile, Leicester were at home to Sheffield Wednesday, and the result gave Gordon his first clean sheet in the First Division. Things were looking better. Looking at the first quarter, or a bit less of that season, Leicester City conceded forty goals, in the final three-quarters, or a bit more, they only conceded thirty-five.

In the FA Cup they played four matches. The third round saw a 2-1 defeat to Wrexham away, then a 2-1 home win over Fulham. This was followed in the fifth round with a 2-1 win over West Bromwich Albion at home, but then came a 2-1 defeat by Wolverhampton Wanderers at Molineaux. So with this improvement of goals conceded, Gordon had established himself as the first-team goalkeeper at Leicester City – on only three more occasions did he, or more accurately his team, take a hiding like the Everton game.

But this didn't happen by itself. Gordon would do the usual training with his teammates, but he'd put in a lot of extra work, such as asking players from Leicester's youth team to practice shot-taking against him – he called himself his 'own greatest critic'. Another skill he wanted to master was blocking the chip or lob, and he achieved this.

Fast forwarding a bit to an international at Wembley against the Scots (who else). Denis Law (who else) in plenty of space looked up to see Gordon coming out, so he chipped the ball from about '17 or 18 yards, and it was going over Banks' head. How he got back, I'll never know'. To watch it now, two factors – as well as consummate skill – were anticipation and timing. Tommy Gemmell said the save was on a par with the save made against Pelé. There are similarities, not least of which is the pure pleasure to watch.

Coming back to the end of the 1959/60 season, Leicester City finished sixteenth in the League on thirty-nine points. They won thirteen, drew thirteen and lost sixteen. The second half of the season had seen a big improvement, so optimism was running high at Filbert Street through the close season.

Back in training in late summer, Leicester started off their 1960/61 campaign at home to Blackpool with a 1-1 draw. That season was about one team though – Tottenham Hotspur. Tottenham won the double that year, the first club to do so last century, and they beat Leicester City in the cup final. Tottenham were lucky though, something I'll return to after a brief look at the season.

It was the debut time for the Football League Cup, with Leicester falling to Rotherham at home. Gordon was to win a Football League Cup winners' (not a medal but a) tankard with Leicester a few seasons later, and again in 1972 when the competition had firmly established itself.

For Leicester City, the season of 1960/61 was dominated by the FA Cup. But what seemed significant is the transfer to Leicester of a goalkeeper from Leeds United, George Heyes. This is significant because then Gordon began to feel he was the first-choice goalkeeper, describing

George as an 'understudy'. He wasn't one to rest on his laurels though. In the League they had mixed fortunes, and after drawing at home to Blackpool they beat Chelsea 3-1 at Stamford Bridge. But over the next four games they were defeated four times and let in eleven goals. Matt Gillies made changes and things quickly turned around – their rate for conceding goals fell dramatically and it took the opposing sides eight games to score eleven goals – one could say a 50 per cent improvement. Ken Leek had come into the first team, and up front with Albert Cheesebrough things looked more settled.

They entered the Christmas fixture list with the sour taste of a 5-1 defeat at Blackpool. They lost to Bolton Wanderers 2-0 on Christmas Eve but beat them 2-0 on Boxing Day. On New Year's Eve, Leicester beat Everton 4-1 and then, after a 1-1 draw at Blackburn, they beat Manchester United 6-0 at Filbert Street. Indeed, it wasn't until West Ham beat them by 1-0 on 31 March that Gordon went to the dressing room on a losing side – their last two raids to London had seen them defeat Arsenal 3-1 and the League leaders and eventual champions Tottenham Hotspur at White Hart Lane. Three days after the West Ham defeat, the two lined up against each other again at home, and Leicester beat them 5-1! But it was the Tottenham match that grabbed the headlines – and they were big headlines too.

More than twice as many people who had braved the Merseyside drizzle about fifteen months earlier filed through the White Hart Lane turnstiles on Saturday 4 February 1961 to see Leicester City beat all-conquering Tottenham Hotspur 3-2. That season Tottenham scored more than twice as many goals as they conceded.

As the season progressed, so did the FA Cup competition. On 7 January 1961, they were drawn at home to Oxford United – still a non-League side and whom Leicester dispatched 3-1. At home to Bristol City on 31 January, they eased past them 5-1. In the fifth round they crossed the Midlands to St Andrews in Birmingham – that was a tough match, though Leicester squeezed through after a replay at Filbert Street. Then they were to meet Barnsley, a Third Division side who they wisely didn't underestimate. At Filbert Street the tie was goalless, but when the replay went to extra time the Leicester players must have been relieved to see Howard Riley score – but that was soon cancelled out by Barnsley's Ken Oliver. Ken Leek scored the winner, and that must have saved many a City fan from blood-pressure problems!

In the semi-finals, Leicester were drawn against Sheffield United, a Second Division side. They gave them a run for their money on neutral ground in Leeds and the tie was goalless. At the City Ground in Nottingham, the replay was again goalless. So off they all trudged to St Andrews in Birmingham for a second replay – Leicester's sixth match that month, two of which went to extra time. Both Leicester and Sheffield United missed penalties, but Jimmy Walsh and Ken Leek wrapped the game up for Leicester at 2-0. So Leicester City were in the FA Cup final.

There was a seventh game for them in March when they travelled to Upton Park to be beaten 1-0 and their first defeat since Christmas Eve – eighteen games in total! Leicester City were only beaten again once in the League that season when Manchester City came a-hunting. By May, Tottenham were League champions. The League and FA Cup double hadn't been achieved in the twentieth century; in 1957, Manchester United won the League but didn't succeed at Wembley, even with the complete Busby Babes showcase on display.

What didn't help Leicester was a decision by Matt Gillies to drop star striker Ken Leek and for Hugh McIlmoyle to deputise. There are two possible reasons for this. Matt said it was his form, but in the previous ten games Leicester scored twenty-two goals, an above-average strike rate. Ken Leek only played in four of those games and scored in three – over the season he played in forty League and cup games in which he bagged twenty-five goals – so 'form' is questionable, to say the least. Ken had gone out for a drink on the Wednesday night, which Matt saw as a breach of explicit instructions. If this was the reason Ken was dropped, then the punishment was on all the team and, as importantly, the supporters. This and a huge piece of bad luck affected the outcome of the FA Cup final – not to take anything away from Tottenham; their goals were superb. And Hugh McIlmoyle didn't let Leicester, or himself, down.

For the first fifteen minutes or so little happened, then Hugh found Howard Riley on the right wing. The centre saw Peter Baker 'risking life and limb' to clear for Tottenham and they were lucky not to be a goal down. Within a few minutes, disaster hit Leicester. Les Allen and Len Chalmers challenged for a ball – a perfectly good challenge, but Len was hurt, badly. It turned out he tore ligaments in his knee and he should have gone off, but there were no substitutes in those days. So a reshuffle of Leicester saw Howard Riley drop back on the right wing and Frank McLintock take over at right-back. Len went out on the wing and hobbled until about the eightieth minute, when finally he called it a day. And with Hugh McIlmoyle facing the best centre-half in the country – Maurice Norman – the odds had lengthened against Leicester. But with Colin Appleton having a great time in midfield and Albert Cheesebrough supporting Hugh in attack, Tottenham had a fight.

Tottenham's John White found Bobby Smith on the right; Les Allen on the end of it was almost assisted by Richie Norman putting into his own net. Up front no less than four players lined up to take a pop at goal for Leicester, but both teams lacked bite. Gordon said in his autobiography that Ken Leek would have caused problems to Maurice Norman; Hugh lacked experience, not ability, while Maurice had both. Tottenham though were not taking command of the game, and neither goalkeeper was seriously troubled.

A promising counter-attack from Tottenham saw a John White and Terry Dyson one-two, before Colin Appleton took the ball. Danny Blanchflower to John White, who centred for an offside Terry Dyson to find the net. If Tottenham did manage to put a cross in, then Gordon was equal to it. It was no good looking to Bobby Smith, the England centre-forward, as Ian King for Leicester was there.

Half-time: 0-0.

There was more edge to the start of the second half. Leicester took the initiative when Albert Cheesebrough put Hugh McIlmoyle through, but Tottenham's Peter Baker was there.

Howard Riley again broke through, but Ron Henry intercepted and Tottenham countered again. The understanding in the Tottenham attack, which saw them score so many goals that season, just wasn't showing and attacks petered out. Ken Keyworth gave them a corner with a perfectly timed tackle, but Gordon took the ball commandingly. As usual the ball was quickly thrown out to the flank where it was expected, and Leicester's counter-attack through Jimmy Walsh saw the midfielder pass two Tottenham Trojans before the whistle went. From the free-kick, Hugh McIlmoyle's header went nowhere.

Any time Tottenham looked dangerous, the Leicester defence were equal to it, and vice versa. Danny Blanchflower took a free-kick, but right in front of goal Les Allen sliced the ball out for a throw-in! Cliff Jones made a 60-yard run, beating two Leicester men, before Les Allen took the ball and brought Terry Dyson in from the left; he shot straight at Gordon. There were several times when Hugh McIlmoyle won the ball with his sheer determination but he couldn't make it count.

Slowly, the limitations on Len Chalmers and the extra work this created began to show, and Tottenham looked more in control. But Colin Appleton came alive and Howard Riley moved up a gear. Terry Dyson set up a chance for Bobby Smith, Frank McLintock covering, and Gordon couldn't quite get to it – Frank finished up in the net as the ball went wide. Howard Riley on the counter, cut inside and tried to place his shot past Bill Brown from the edge of the 18-yard box, but it went just wide.

John White centred for Gordon to pull the ball down and throw out to the flanks. Howard Riley was away again and his centre saw Bill Brown in the Tottenham goal thwart the two converging Leicester men. A challenge to Cliff Jones just outside the Leicester 18-yard box, and the free-kick was sent out to John White, who centred. Bobby Smith at the far post headed back across the goal and Terry Dyson headed just over from just about 6 yards, 'one of the few times Spurs have been able to open up this brilliant Leicester defence'.

Tottenham were soon in possession again. John White just inside the Leicester half to Bobby Smith, then Cliff Jones to Terry Dyson – fluent football – out to Les Allen on the right and in to Terry Dyson. Whether his was a shot or a pass didn't matter; Bobby Smith took it on his right foot, on the turn, and for once an inch or two away from Ian King – his right-footed shot flew past Gordon. A superbly taken goal.

Leicester were rattled and from the kick-off a few passes went astray, but Howard Riley was off again down the right wing, a long ball to the goal line and a corner. Ian King came up, but Bill Brown in the Tottenham goal took the ball masterfully. Jimmy Walsh was felled by Peter Baker and from the free-kick the ball rolled to Frank McLintock, who shot just wide.

The second Tottenham goal was a second tragedy for Len Chalmers. His pass was intercepted and ran loose to Bobby Smith, who laid it off to John White and then back. Bobby looked up, Gordon was at his near post and so he had plenty of time to take the ball to the goal line before crossing. Gordon charged across the goal, but Terry Dyson was there first with almost a free header as Gordon collided spectacularly with his far post, and with fourteen minutes of the match left Tottenham were two goals up.

Leicester's determination seemed almost tangible; Len Chalmers finally limped off ten minutes from time. Howard Riley led an attack again but Bill Brown was equal to it. Frank McLintock sent another through ball towards Howard, but Dave Mackay intercepted. A Tottenham attack ensued. Bobby Smith laid the ball off to Terry Dyson, but his shot went straight to Gordon; Cliff Jones repeated the feat in the next Tottenham attack. Danny Blanchflower put the ball through to John White, who crossed, but Colin Appleton almost danced the ball out of trouble. Ian King won the ball in his own half and travelled up with it, laying it off and getting it back and laying it off again. Goal kick.

The final whistle gave Tottenham a unique celebration.

The presentations were made, but Len Chalmers didn't come out for his medal, although the following season he was back fully fit for Leicester.

Back in training in late summer, Leicester started off their 1961/62 campaign at Manchester City, but were beaten 3-1. This didn't really improve that much over the months, and the season was only punctuated by Leicester City's first taste of European football. As runners-up to the double-winning Tottenham, who qualified for the European Cup, Leicester were automatic qualifiers for the European Cup Winners' Cup. They cruised past Irish club Glenavon away and at home, before dropping a very late goal to Athletico Madrid in the next round. The second leg in Madrid saw them depart from the competition – Gordon saved one penalty but not the next. Athletico went on to win the competition.

Leicester's Saturday afternoon and associated business saw them struggle a bit with their form, and some rather ghastly scorelines came up against them. They departed from the Football League Cup in the first round and the FA Cup in the third.

Tottenham attempted to strengthen their position as League champions and FA Cup holders when they signed Jimmy Greaves from the Italian club AC Milan. Denis Law had tasted Italian League football and found it was too defensive – Jimmy was later to say of his time in Italy that he 'hated every minute of it'. Tottenham didn't win the League for a second successive season, the accolade went to East Anglia where Ipswich Town, under Mr (as he was then) Alf Ramsey, fought long and hard to win it. They were not everyone's idea of League champions, but in football every goal and every victory counts. And Alf was, Gordon was to later say, a great strategist who could also motivate players. It's more usual for teams who are well motivated to become confident, which leads to an upward spiral rather than a downward. But no matter how much one praises a manager, it's what the players with their twenty-two feet and eleven heads do.

Ken Leek left Leicester, which isn't surprising, and I'd love to have said he hit the real big-time, but he didn't.

In the final shout Leicester finished in mid-table – fourteenth – with forty points from seventeen wins and six draws. They were beaten on nineteen occasions and some of the scorelines are not to their great credit. In goal, Gordon played forty-one of the forty-two League games that season – he didn't play in their game against Tottenham at White Hart Lane – and pulled the ball from his goal on seventy occasions, but that isn't as bad as it sounds; he kept ten clean sheets. And the England squad, still under Walter Winterbottom, sought his services, although he didn't play – Ron Springett kept a clean sheet against Portugal in a 2-0 victory, but everyone was talking about their young star, Eusébio.

Before moving on, it is of interest to look at a development (or perhaps a non-development) in professional football in the early 1960s.

I always thought that Shakespeare was the first to say 'money was the root of all evil', and he probably would have if the New Testament didn't make the point first. The world has changed since Biblical times, and since Shakespeare's time too, and more recently, say in the past few decades since the end of the Second World War, two notable issues from the money side of football have come about. The first is falling attendances, but falling attendances doesn't necessarily mean less people see the game, it simply means fewer are standing on the terraces at the grounds; or more recently, fewer people were sitting in the stadia. So it's possible that just as many people love football now as did in the immediate post-war period, but they're in armchairs at home, or perhaps they're in the pub. So it's difficult to be decisive, and it's not an important issue.

But the second issue I want to discuss is players' wages. Although the 'business' of football has changed, in the start it was an amateur pursuit; then, towards the end of the nineteenth century, the FA allowed clubs to employ professional players. But as soon as the century turned, a wage cap was introduced of £4 per week, and the players rightly thought they should form a representative body to enhance their rights, though the FA soon wanted a ban on such a body.

But wages did rise and by the end of the First World War, the pay was approaching £9 a week. It's not easy to draw a comparison with today's prices as retail prices and average earnings are calculated differently, but £9 a week was above the average, though wages were to fall again in the 1920s.

After the Second World War, the National Arbitration Tribunal raised players' wages to £12 per week. All of this was for the season only, and many players received little in the summer months. However, the principle of raises became regular and the £14 cap in 1951 rose steadily to £20 per week in 1958, but it was the clubs who benefited most from the post-war attendance boom.

The Professional Footballers' Association (PFA) was growing in strength. With the appointment of the (to say the least) versatile and articulate Jimmy Hill as chairman, the cast was complete for a showdown with the FA. On 14 January 1961, the threat of a strike effectively finished the era of the maximum wage – on that day Leicester City and Blackburn Rovers played at Ewood Park, with both sides scoring two goals. Brian Clough, then a Middlesbrough player, was quoted to have said, 'I would expect the right to negotiate my contract the same as any other profession.'

A contemporary of Brian's put the matter in the hands of lawyers though. George Eastham was a Newcastle United player whose contract had come to an end, and in 1959 the refusal of a player to enter into a further contract with a club meant the club could hold on to their registration and simply stop paying them. Arsenal saved the day by paying a huge £47,500 for George, but the litigation continued. But George wanted to earn a living and Newcastle United, or more accurately their manager Charlie Mitten, was refusing him that right. Lord Wilberforce adjudged that any player out of contract being restricted from taking up employment elsewhere was a restraint of trade. So George Eastham was the star, though the court appearances would have been difficult for him – and it nearly bankrupted the PFA.

George Eastham was really a 'great', and like his dad played for England! There are not many of those. He played seventeen times and was in the squad both for the 1962 and 1966 World Cup finals but didn't play. He did play at Wembley in 1972 though, when he, Gordon and nine others lifted the Football League Cup! Needless to say, I'll talk about George some more.

Fulham chairman Tommy Trinder, who was a professional comedian, had quipped that he should be able to pay his best player (Johnny Haynes) £100 a week, so, thereafter, he had to! And it wasn't long before there was a £1,000 a week player, whose identity will surprise no one – George Best. John Barnes of Liverpool became the first player to reach £10,000 a week, and the 'Bosman Ruling' – giving players free transfers at the end of their contracts – and the right they now acquired to negotiate their wages, pushed the figures up again. As to what the top players are now paid, that's a matter for another day!

5

The Nation Calls

Future England manager Walter Winterbottom was born in Oldham in Lancashire in 1913. He began playing football as a youth and joined Mossley in the Cheshire League at the end of the 1934/35 season, and signed amateur forms. He was a strong and skilful centre-half, and became a regular selection; Manchester United soon signed him up. His debut came in 1936 when George Vose was injured. But although considered hot property, Walter's career came to an end the following season when he was diagnosed with a spinal disease (ankylosing spondylitis). He was a schoolteacher by profession so could concentrate on this, but he also enrolled as a student at Carnegie Physical Education College, subsequently joining the staff there. Just before the Second World War, the FA ran seminars and conferences and he met Sir Stanley Rous and other top FA officials.

The war intervened and Walter joined the RAF, where he rose to Wing Commander before taking up an appointment with the FA when the war ended. The role was effectively as England's manager, a post he held from 1946 to 1962. He set up the under-23 team, but a panel made the team selection – he had virtually no power at all in shaping a team for any major victories, although he took England to four World Cup final tournaments. The concept of selection panels was soon to change, but in the years following the war this was the set-up. Slowly though, things did change and the panel later became a smaller pool of three, so Walter only had two others to convince of his preferred player.

In the spring of 1961, Leicester City were enjoying a good FA Cup run, which took them to Wembley to meet the mighty Tottenham Hotspur. But another little accolade was to come their way – their goalkeeper was called up for the England under-23 squad and he won two caps, against Wales and then against Scotland. This was under the tenure of Walter Winterbottom.

On Wednesday 8 February 1961, the England under-23 team took to the pitch at Goodison Park in Liverpool in front of a crowd of 27,000-odd spectators and beat their Welsh counterparts 2-0.

So Gordon had taken the step up to international football – but this night it was Welsh goalkeeper Dave Hollins of Brighton who stole the show. He was on top form in the first half, and made at least three saves from shots that could have made England unbeatable: his best effort was a one-handed save from a Bobby Moore diving header. He was beaten eventually though by a thirty-minute penalty, driven home by inside-right Chris Crowe. Left-winger Clive Clark had been brought down by Ollie Burton. Ollie had dropped back to play at right-back instead of centre-forward because Brian Hughes had been forced out on the right-wing through a thigh muscle injury. Shortly after the penalty, Clive Clark forced Dave Hollins to make another diving save from his header. Centre-half Mel Nurse was solid in defence and kept Wales out of more trouble, and subdued centre-forward Johnny Byrne with some incisive tackles.

England dominated the game in midfield and Wales didn't have a shot on goal for just over the first half-hour. But they settled down to some good football, and eventually Herbie Williams struck from 25 yards – Gordon forced the ball out for a corner.

The interesting point about writing a biography of a goalkeeper is if the defence are working well then the goalkeeper is redundant, so all the action and reporting comes from the other end!

Les Allen finished the first half with a good move but was thwarted again by more fine goalkeeping from Dave Hollins. Arfon Griffiths, the new and brief star at Arsenal, came on at the start of the second half, and almost scored when outside-left Freddie Jones put him through. Wales began to look more dangerous, Arfon nodded down a right-wing cross in the fifty-third minute, but it was too close to Gordon and it didn't stretch him.

In the sixty-third minute, England struck again when Mel Nurse brought Les Allen down just outside the 18-yard box and Bobby Moore's free-kick was deflected in by a defender, although one commentator described Bobby's free-kick as taken 'Puskas-style': perhaps Bobby taught more than we thought!

Right-winger Barrie Jones seemed to mount a one-man attack; beating two defenders before his shot went wide. A further strike followed within minutes and then another brought a fine save from Gordon. Two late assaults were made on the Welsh goal when Johnny Byrne sent Les Allen scuttling forward, but he shot wide and wing-half John Kirkham joined in an England move to take a return pass before shooting straight at Dave Hollins.

So England finished comfortable, but not exciting winners, with a penalty and a free-kick to nil; though on the more positive side, there were five new caps that night. And two players who would become household names shone – Bobby Moore and Gordon Banks.

As I mentioned, the Leicester City team had a very good season in 1960/61, but the stars were undoubtedly Tottenham after their double. Their first home defeat, only their third defeat all season, was in early February when Gordon and his side won 3-2 at White Hart Lane – this was the Saturday before the under-23 fixture of above, so would have done wonders for Gordon's confidence. Leicester were a good side and in the First Division finished a good sixth that year, so the future looked rosy. And with his first cap under his belt, Gordon keenly looked forward to his next England under-23 game.

On 1 March, the squad took on a Scotland under-23 side at Ayresome Park in Middlesbrough, where the Scots took the advantage due to a perfect striker; one Gordon would meet time and time again – Denis Law. But the England defence were reshuffled and in came a young right-back from Fulham, George Cohen. He was joined by Mick McNeil, who was captain and playing on his home ground. Everton's Brian Labone and Bobby Moore completed the back four.

The press were heavily critical of the youngsters' performances, but wading through the match reports one finds plenty of criticism of the forward line, but barely a mention of the defence, in a critical sense at any rate. The Scottish strikers though were praised, 'steely determination … of Denis Law'. John McLeod and Dave Hilley both created chances with 'cool, neat approach work'. So why didn't they score more than the single goal?

On the subject of the goal, however, it was the three aforementioned who combined to make it happen: a cross from Dave Hilley onto Denis Law's head was cleared by Gordon, only for John McLeod to cross the ball from the other side, which saw Denis fire in a low, hard shot that sufficed to record the victory.

It was suggested that England were 'jittery around the penalty area'. And Mick McNeil cleared off the line when 'Banks was all at sea'. But there was not a critical mention of the back four. Until Alan Gilzean connected with a corner and Mick McNeil thumped the ball off the line: Denis Law missed the penalty. John Kirkham from midfield brought out the best save from John Ogston in the Scotland goal, shortly after clearing off his own goal line. Football is about scoring goals, and stopping them, but with far too much criticism of the front runners, a clear picture was elusive.

Gordon only played two games for the under-23 side, but it looks more likely that his age was the reason he only played the two games.

Within two years of the Wales and Scotland game, Walter had left the England job and the FA appointed a manager who had laid it down as a requisite that the manager alone would select the team; the FA acquiesced.

Alfred Ramsey was born in Dagenham in Essex in 1920, and played as a full-back for Southampton and later Tottenham Hotspur as well as England's national side. But this man was as much an enigma as he was astute. He could see in his playing days that football management offered much reward, but he needed to do two things: replace his broad London accent (I wonder if he would now – I should hope not), and develop a reticence that was, unfortunately, almost universally misunderstood as aloofness. He knew England had the players to win a World Cup, but what could he do with his squad that Walter didn't? The answer was quite simple and Alf (and his trainer Harold Shepherdson) knew what it was. He needed to get to know the players, and that meant a 'hands-on' approach, almost a 'family' atmosphere. He wanted to immerse himself in the football and not the media circus or politics. And he knew it would take a while to build a strong team. As a full-back, he knew he would need a solid defence – including a goalkeeper. If any proof was needed, Alf needed only to refer to his own days when England were beaten 6-3 by Hungary in 1953, and 7-1 the following year.

With the No. 1 jersey heading Gordon's way in the full England squad, Alf knew he had a solid goal-line defence, and he knew about defence line-ups. However, football is fickle and one can't look too far into the future. Maurice Norman was a stalwart as centre-half, and Gordon felt confident with him, but he broke a leg in a friendly match. George Cohen and Ray Wilson were hovering around and sometimes together, and Bobby Moore was a mainstay. It's possible Maurice would have been around for a while if he hadn't broken his leg, but Alf needed a strong centre-half, and when he selected Jack Charlton he had the four defenders and the goalkeeper good enough to lift the World Cup.

6

Leicester City
The Middle Years

Gordon had now established himself as one of the top goalkeepers in the country, but continued to train hard and carefully consider his performances. He knew that one important factor in playing football was to concentrate wholly on the game. It's surprising how quickly a counter-attack can come, and many goalkeepers have been caught on the hop by a quick breakaway.

By the end of April 1962, the most unlikely League champions were on their throne – Alf Ramsey's Ipswich Town. They have been called some unflattering names and labelled as dull, but that season they scored ninety-three goals, which was only bettered by their runners-up, Burnley. The Lancashire side beat them 4-3 at Turf Moor, but a week later the scoreline was Ipswich Town six Burnley two! Ipswich did the double over League champions Tottenham Hotspur, and Gordon had to retrieve the ball from his net three times – once at Portman Road and then again twice at Filbert Street – as a double was also recorded against Leicester.

In the summer of 1962, all eyes were on South America where the World Cup finals were to be held. England finished as runners-up in Group Four to Hungary – Brazil beat England 3-1 in the quarter-finals, and later beat Czechoslovakia by the same scoreline in the final. Gordon didn't go to Chile and Walter Winterbottom opted for Ron Springett with his Sheffield neighbour (at United), Alan Hodgkinson as understudy – Alan didn't actually play. The first-choice centre-half for England was Peter Swann, who didn't play due to illness, but due to another slip he also made the headlines following his side's (Sheffield Wednesday) defeat at Ipswich in December.

Ipswich didn't repeat their success the following season, and Leicester City didn't look likely champions either, even with new signings made at the end of the previous season – Mike Stringfellow was a young and speedy winger who came from Mansfield Town, and Davie Gibson came down from Hibernian.

Leicester City started with a defeat at Fulham, but then started to put a good string of results together; only losing 3-2 against Everton in September, and in October they only lost one match, a 2-1 defeat at Blackburn Rovers. And they were only defeated once in December when Fulham won 3-2.

On 8 January 1963, in bitterly cold conditions, Leicester beat Grimsby Town at their Blundell Park ground 3-1. Ken Keyworth opened the scoring, and Davie Gibson added two goals. The weather put Leicester out of business again until three weeks later when Ipswich Town came up to Filbert Street in the FA Cup fourth round, where Leicester turned out winners 3-1. Leicester were also in fourth place in the League, just six points behind Tottenham Hotspur. So they're in the fifth round of the FA Cup and flying high in the First Division.

In February and March as the fixture backlog built up, they were not to be defeated again until a trip to West Ham in April. During that time, Gordon kept nine clean sheets and when they did let a goal in – against Everton in February – it was the only goal. Jimmy Greaves scored in the 2-2 draw in March, but by then Leicester looked good for the double! They'd beaten Leyton Orient by a goal to nil at Brisbane Road in the sixth round of the FA Cup and they were second in the First Division, having only conceded thirty-two goals; only three more than Everton, but Leicester City were a better strike force.

Gordon's form was running at full whack, and Jimmy Greaves, one of the League's all-time highest scorers, said it was a job to get the ball past him.

On 30 March, they beat Norwich City to reach the semi-finals of the FA Cup. And with less than a dozen League games left, the double still looked a possibility. They beat Orient away 2-0 but could only draw at Blackpool, but they were second in the League and joint first in their defensive record. At Upton Park, West Ham beat them 2-0 – and it would seem this wasn't a struggle for Bobby Moore and his men. Leicester only earned, it seems, 'an odd round of polite applause' as West Ham took the game over. That morning Leicester City had stood on top of the First Division with West Ham in fourteenth place, but Alan Sealey pounced twice. The first goal came as a strange and 'overly optimistic appeal for a penalty' made the Leicester defenders pull up, Alan stroked the ball past Gordon with apparent ease. The pen of Clement Freud reported, 'Banks was as impressive as ever, providing a moment of gladness when he ran out to a long ball that failed to carry into his penalty area and calmly heading it back over the advancing Hurst.'

With West Ham two goals up, Leicester were described as 'inferior' and they slipped to fourth in the League. They played Manchester United twice in two days, drawing at Old Trafford two goals each and then defeating them the following day 4-3 at Filbert Street. They were now on fifty-one points and back on top of the table, but Tottenham Hotspur and Everton were both on fifty points, and both had a game in hand.

On 20 April, Wolverhampton Wanderers took a point in a 1-1 draw against Leicester. Everton beat Tottenham 1-0, and it looked as though this might have won the Merseyside team the League championship, but Everton and Tottenham still had five games to go.

On 27 April, Everton went to West Ham and won 2-1, and Liverpool travelled to Hillsborough to take on Leicester City in the FA Cup semi-final. However, it wasn't an exciting affair with both teams adopting a defence and then quick-break tactics, which didn't really suit either. Mike Stringfellow scored the only goal of the game after twenty minutes, while Gordon occupied himself when Ian Callaghan crossed to perfection, but no one was on the end of it. Roger Hunt hit the crossbar a few minutes later before he hit a shot on the half turn, which brought about a fine save. Ron Yeats was placed in the centre-forward position and was magnificent. But Leicester ran for the safety of the dressing room to hear Gordon's demon Denis Law had scored for Manchester United at Villa Park to defeat Southampton in the other semi-final.

On 4 May, Leicester City lost to West Bromwich Albion at The Hawthorns, which effectively finished their championship hopes – Everton had won at home to Bolton Wanderers and so were now five points clear of Leicester. Three more defeats awaited them but Gordon didn't play any further League games that season, and the list of injuries included Gordon, Mike Stringfellow, Davie Gibson and Ian King. Leicester City finished fourth and the championship went to Everton, who won their final four matches.

But they had a fixture on 25 May, which could mean a trophy was heading to Filbert Street – the FA Cup final. They were against a Manchester United side with Denis Law, the most expensive footballer in the country, and former golden boy Albert Quixall. Noel Cantwell was at the back and his fellow countryman Johnny Giles was in midfield. Bobby Charlton of course featured, as did David Herd and Pat Crerand. Manchester United had not had a good season and had finished in nineteenth place, just two points above Manchester City, who were relegated. Since the Munich crash they hadn't won any trophies.

But it was a joyous week for Leicester City: Colin and Sheila Appleton welcomed their daughter Deborah into the world; Frank and Barbara McLintock welcomed their son Neil; and Ursula Banks gave birth to Wendy. What a week. A goodbye, but not a sad one, was said to Ken Aston, who refereed his last match that day at Wembley, but his service to football and refereeing was to continue.

The game got underway after Prince Phillip had met the teams, and it was lively from the start. After about ten minutes an intelligent through ball from Denis Law, catching three Leicester players, just failed to connect with Albert Quixall and rolled into Gordon's arms. As usual he was to throw the ball out for the quick counter, and it reached Ken Keyworth just about on the halfway line! Ken flicked on to Mike Stringfellow, who managed to beat Bill Foulkes and Pat Crerand and he almost made the goal line before sending the ball right across the face of the goal with David Gaskell beaten – fortunately for Manchester United Noel Cantwell was just goal-side of Ken Keyworth. The time from when the ball left Gordon and reached Ken, who could make a scoring attempt, was an amazing thirteen seconds!

Mike Stringfellow had a lot of aerial play, and at one time towered above David Gaskell at about 3 yards from goal – Richie Norman had taken a free-kick for Leicester just inside the United half, it was flicked on, or back, and David Gaskell's punch rescued United. But the ball found its way out to Howard Riley on the right, whose centre put the goal under threat again before the ball was cleared – when the ball was again played back in, Mike Stringfellow was offside.

The future Leeds superstar Johnny Giles played well that day, and one particular move saw Pat Crerand send a perfect ball to him on the right wing – he dribbled up and passed a couple of Leicester players before making one of the most perfect passes with the outside of his right foot, which saw Denis Law get into a great goalscoring position. Gordon had read it and was quickly off his line to halt the attack.

Denis Law laid on an almost perfect goalscoring chance to Bobby Charlton, but he struck the ball wide. From the goal kick, Graham Cross won possession and chipped a ball right over the Manchester United defence to Davie Gibson, but David Gaskell just got there first. He lost it but fortunately Tony Dunne was there to feed Noel Cantwell and the ball went out of defence and into the Leicester 18-yard box where Bobby Charlton set up Johnny Giles – goal kick. When Ken Wolstenholme discussed the 'quick switch' of the game he was right. Pat Crerand shot from a distance and Gordon reminded his defence they had a job to do!

The Leicester City defence began to look a little raggedy, and Manchester United continued to probe. Johnny Giles sailed in a corner, but Gordon took it quite confidently. He'd given his defenders a bit of a pep talk/shout and this settled them a little.

On the break Leicester were still dangerous, Davie Gibson played a high ball into the Manchester United 18-yard box for Ken Keyworth to lay off: Mike Stringfellow just couldn't get there in time.

Noel Cantwell came up on the overlap, but Bobby Charlton played the ball in to David Herd, who passed it on to Denis Law, who played it on to Bobby Charlton – on his right foot – but the shot lacked the usual power and it went straight at Gordon. But Leicester were not getting the ball out of the danger zone. From Gordon's throw, Davie Gibson didn't get to the ball in time and Pat Crerand took possession. He accelerated into the Leicester City 18-yard box. David Herd and Denis Law were to his right in plenty of space. The ball went to Denis and on the turn he shot low and hard: 1-0. Gordon was furious at his defenders and he seemed to have a good point.

Manchester United were not going to rest on their laurels. Gordon took a good cross from Noel Cantwell before the ubiquitous Denis Law could get his head to it. Denis to David Herd and back – Denis was through and on to Gordon, whom he dribbled around to find himself on the corner of the 6-yard box. With Gordon helpless, Denis found four Leicester City defenders around him to stop the ball crossing the goal line. Gordon had no complaints about that and the idea that he was master of his 18-yard box – barking when he needed to had produced the right responses.

Manchester United remained a goal up at half-time.

Leicester City started the second half with a little more bite, and Gordon's first touch was a goal kick. Manchester United settled as the more attacking side, and Gordon took a cross easily as Denis Law challenged.

Twelve minutes into the second half, David Gaskell took a cross and quickly threw it out to Johnny Giles on the right – he dribbled upfield unchallenged, and just over the halfway line he found Bobby Charlton on the left flank. He took the ball up to the edge of the 18-yard box – Gordon had come out a bit and was on his 6-yard line. Bobby shot and it looked as though John Sjoberg blocked Gordon's vision, and a ball one would usually expect him to save rolled through to David Herd to tap it right-footed into the empty goal. So, 2-0.

From the restart, Graham Cross shot at the other end and was only a couple of inches wide.

Taking the ball out of defence, Pat Crerand found Johnny Giles again on the right, who put forward an inch-perfect pass to Denis Law, but Gordon had read the situation and was soon off his line. Albert Quixall shot from 30 yards that Gordon easily dealt with.

Unusually, Gordon was penalised, seemingly for a handball as he had taken a pace or half a pace out of the 18-yard box for a clearance. From the free-kick, Noel Cantwell headed well wide. David Gaskell in the Manchester United goal had a shot or two to save, and one from Frank McLintock nearly crept in.

About ten minutes from time Ken Keyworth headed home in quite spectacular fashion following a shot from Frank McLintock. Bobby Charlton made a pass of about 70 yards that found Denis Law, who then passed to David Herd, who crossed perfectly for Denis to head the ball against the post – it bounced straight back into Gordon's hands.

'Five minutes to go – it's all over now,' was Ken Wolstenholme's comment when a long cross from Johnny Giles found Gordon, who uncharacteristically fumbled the ball and it fell at David Herd's feet for his second goal.

Full time: Manchester United three, Leicester City one, both Matt Gillies and Colin Appleton said the best team won.

Gordon and Ursula Banks spent the summer – the close season – as new parents with Wendy; Robert was by now approaching his fifth birthday.

The season of 1963/64 got off to a good start for Leicester and they had signed Bobby Roberts for the then huge fee of £41,000. Gordon had worked hard at the back end of the Leicester field to stop the opponents cancelling out the forwards' efforts. Over the seasons, the amount of goals conceded when Gordon was in attendance dropped – though he is keen to point out this was because of team factors. But he practiced and experimented in just about every way he could, from short shots in the 6-yard box to the best way to cover a corner. And in covering corners, it was how the opposition could be stopped by using defenders tactically, and it was the forwards waiting to take the ball away from a long throw – goals from a counter-attack are always more likely to catch the opposition on the hop, especially if taller air-able defenders have come up for the setpiece. Bobby Moore was said to know in advance what a player was going to do, and it seemed as though Gordon was to follow suit – he called it a 'journey of self-discovery'. It would be worth it, as the best strikers in the world were left scratching their head and the gasps from spectators were always audible on television, on the rare occasion when the commentator could hold himself; but televised football was still a rarity.

Leicester's first match of the 1963/64 campaign was a 1-1 draw against West Bromwich Albion away, followed by a convincing 3-0 win against Birmingham City at Filbert Street. Following this was a 7-2 defeat of Arsenal, and everyone wondered if Leicester City would be there among the top teams again that season. It wasn't to be – Gordon suggested later that it was the unsteady form. The FA Cup was as bad for them, and they went out of the competition in the third round 3-2 at Leyton Orient.

But there was to be a success for Leicester that season in the young companion to the FA Cup, the Football League Cup. This was a relatively new competition, although some clubs were a bit reluctant – European competitions were also a fairly new addition to many clubs fixtures, often with home and away legs, and another domestic competition may clog up the season's fixture list. It was a strong argument, and it was supported by the big freeze over the 1962/63 season. But eventually the Football League Cup won through and is still competed.

It was originally thought of by Sir Stanley Rouse, though it was Alan Hardakre who actually got the competition up and running. Most grounds had floodlights by the late 1950s, bar the odd exception, and so midweek evening football became a possibility. Aston Villa were the first winners of the Football League Cup, and the final was over two – home and away. Later the final became a one-off match at Wembley, and Gordon's CV will cover both.

It was on 25 September that Leicester took on the Fourth Division's Aldershot at Filbert Street in front of a crowd of 9,500-odd, and goals from Bob Newton and Ken Keyworth were enough. Three weeks later, they travelled north to beat Tranmere Rovers 2-1 – Billy Hodgson and Bobby Roberts were on target and entertained a crowd of nearly 13,000. Against Gillingham in the last week of November, Ken Keyworth was on top form, scoring one and creating the chances for Frank McLintock and Billy Hodgson. A crowd of 10,356 saw Gordon have a good game, and George Francis got a consolation goal for the visitors. Gordon had saved an earlier effort and had tipped a strike from Ron Newman over the bar – Ron was later manager of Fort Lauderdale Strikers, who Gordon played for in the late 1970s.

Gordon didn't play in the fifth-round 1-1 tie at Norwich, and deputy George Heyes made a 'wonderful' save in the last minute to bring the clubs to Filbert Street in mid-January.

Leicester won 2-1: Howard Riley and Billy Hodgson, which cancelled out a Graham Cross own goal. Gordon didn't have a lot to do! In the semi-final, 14,000-odd folk saw West Ham beaten 4-3, and Leicester had been 4-1 up at one point. Alan Sealy late and Geoff Hurst for the Hammers answered Ken Keyworth, Bobby Roberts, Mike Stringfellow and Frank McLintock. West Ham looked good for the second leg at Upton Park and one reporter commented that it was 'method against method'. It was a good match with Frank McLintock and Bobby Roberts giving Leicester a win and the crowd saw 'Gordon Banks in the form that has made him England's number one'. Attendance was 27,329.

The first leg of the final at The Victoria Ground saw a 1-1 draw, with Keith Bebbington's goal for Stoke City cancelled out by Davie Gibson two minutes from time. But the second leg was a 3-2 cracker, with Mike Stringfellow, Davie Gibson and Howard Riley netting for Leicester, and Dennis Viollet and, in the last seconds, George Kinnell replying for Stoke. 'Gordon Banks produced his best England form. Three fantastic saves … from John Ritchie.' So the Football League Cup was going to Leicester, and finally Gordon received a winner's trophy.

It was a sad time for Gordon and everyone wearing football boots that year because the big betting scandal hit the headlines. Only a few players were involved, but it tarnished the game. Gordon's old schoolmate David (Bronco) Lane was found guilty and sent away with two other Sheffield Wednesday players (though Tony Kay had gone to Everton), which was punishment in excess. They received life bans. but those were lifted in 1972. Jimmy Gauld was the ringleader.

The 1964/65 season started for Leicester with a trip up to Roker Park to take on the newly promoted Sunderland. The match finished with three goals each, George Mulhall gave Sunderland the lead in the third minute with a 20-yard drive that seemed to catch the Leicester defence unaware. Leicester looked the more enterprising side, but Derek Forster, a fifteen-year-old from the youth team, kept Leicester at bay with some fine goalkeeping. Mike Stringfellow got the equaliser and Tom Sweenie put Leicester in front. George Herd equalised and George Mulhall restored Sunderland's lead. Ken Keyworth got the final goal of the afternoon.

Leicester beat Wolverhampton Wanderers at home 3-2 and drew away 1-1 the following week; a 2-2 draw with Manchester United was sandwiched between the two Wolves fixtures. Chelsea came, John Hollins scored to get them a point at one goal each, and then champions Liverpool came to Filbert Street.

The Leicester defence had conceded nine goals in their first five games – they had scored ten, but Gordon would have taken little consolation in that. When the champions came though he kept a clean sheet. Liverpool were not at their best, and only one save from Roger Hunt caused Gordon any anguish.

They were beaten 3-2 away to Leeds, and then by Arsenal at home by the same scoreline. In the Football League Cup they were held to a goalless draw by Peterborough United, though when they went for the replay Leicester were comfortable winners. At Ewood Park, Blackburn Rovers beat them 3-1, and when Blackpool came to Filbert Street the game could have been quite different than the 3-2 scoreline – Gordon made fine saves from Tony Green and Graham Oates.

On 10 October, Leicester travelled to Fulham and met a powerful side – Gordon pulled the ball out of his net on five occasions. It wasn't a happy day for him. In an early attack he botched a catch from a cross from which Fulham nearly went ahead, but when Johnny Haynes hit a 30-yard strike, Gordon didn't catch it cleanly and Pat O'Connell scored. At half-time Fulham led 5-1, and with a final score of 5-2, Matt Gillies must have used some well chosen words at half-time.

In mid-October, Nottingham Forest came to Filbert Street; Gordon sustained a groin strain, and later in a collision with Colin Addison he suffered minor injuries to his face and hands. With an International against Belgium soon after, Gordon said he wasn't too concerned about his fitness. Tottenham Hotspur and Jimmy Greaves came to Leicester and were beaten.

Leicester beat Crystal Palace in the Football League Cup after a replay – Gordon made a great save from a strike of Reg Cutler, and in the replay he was said to make two 'somersault' saves from Cliff Holton.

In three games Leicester conceded eight goals, and in one game they scored eight goals against an injury-hit Coventry City. They'd made the semi-finals of the Football League Cup. In the next four games Leicester only conceded three goals, but it was clear they needed to rebuild their defence – Matt Gillies had been to Cardiff to watch a full-back he wanted to sign, Peter Rodrigues.

As winter took hold, a no-score draw at Upton Park was followed by a 1-0 home defeat by Sunderland. On Boxing Day. Sheffield Wednesday shared the points at two goals each, but two days later at Hillsborough the score was 0-0.

Come the second half of the season; the new year. Leicester City were in the semi-final of the Football League Cup, and with the third round of the FA Cup in January, four of Leicester's seven games in January 1965 were cup-ties. A 4-1 pasting by Chelsea left them reeling and they struggled to get a draw in the FA Cup third round at Filbert Street against Blackburn Rovers: they won the replay 2-1 in a game that 'throbbed throughout with everything that makes football great'. Apparently, Leicester cleared off the line twice, and half a dozen or so other goalscoring attempts missed by inches. But Leicester made their attacks count and were two up at half-time. John Byron pulled one back eleven minutes from time, but it was too late.

Leeds United came down for a 2-2 draw, and to jump a fixture in chronology, Leicester went down 4-3 at Arsenal in a game where the referee escaped thuggery.

On 20 January, Plymouth Argyle, under the management of Malcolm Allison, came to Filbert Street in the first leg of the Football League Cup semi-final. Leicester won 3-2. In the fourth round of the FA Cup, Plymouth Argyle again came to Filbert Street, but this time Leicester City scored all of the five goals.

Blackburn Rovers then won 3-2 at Filbert Street, and four days later Leicester travelled down to Plymouth for the second leg of the Football League Cup semi-final. John Sjoberg scored the only goal of the game in the thirty-sixth minute. For the home side, Mike Trebilcock headed inches wide, and Gordon saved well after a deflection from a Nick Jennings shot. Leicester's defence was solid that night and they were on their way to a second Football League Cup final in two years.

Three days later, Leicester travelled up to Blackpool's Bloomfield Road for a 1-1 draw.

Was a double cup campaign a real possibility in the middle of the 1960s? For the fifth round of the FA Cup, they travelled up to Middlesbrough where they won the game with 'elegant ease'. Poor old Arthur Horsfield didn't take advantage of an open goal about fifteen minutes into the game, and that was about the sum of Middlesbrough's chances.

In the League, they defeated Fulham and were defeated by Nottingham Forest, John Sjoberg misjudging his back pass to give Chris Crowe a gift.

Then the mighty Liverpool came, but the game was nothing mighty, and after a 0-0 washout they all lined up at Anfield four days later. Frank McGhee for the *Daily Mirror* told us, 'Their defence inspired by the brilliance of goalkeeper Gordon Banks cracked just once.' In the seventy-second minute Chris Lawler sent in a free-kick for Ron Yeats to head on for Roger Hunt; he turned and shot with his left foot beyond Gordon's reach.

So no FA Cup that year, and between the defeat by Liverpool and meeting Chelsea in the Football League Cup final, a trip to The Hawthorns at West Bromwich Albion saw Leicester concede six goals without reply.

On 15 March at Stamford Bridge, the first leg of the Football League Cup final took place – at that time Chelsea were League leaders. In the first half Gordon broke his nose, and in the second half he broke his thumb.

Chelsea's Alan Young injured himself when his flying header was superbly saved by Gordon and they collided. A Terry Venables shot got the better of him but Len Chalmers deflected it out of harm's way. A brilliant save followed when he pushed a shot from George Graham over the bar, but Bobby Tambling scored shortly after.

When the second half started, Colin Appleton immediately equalised. Terry Venables converted a penalty and five minutes later Jimmy Goodfellow equalised for Leicester. On centre-forward duty following the reshuffling of Chelsea that night was Eddie McCreadie, who got the winner.

It would have helped Leicester's confidence to beat Sheffield United 2-0 at Brammall Lane, and see Everton off 2-1 at Filbert Street.

Then Chelsea came up for the second leg, but neither team was that hot and the game finished with no goals. Gordon saved superbly from Bobby Tambling. and then smothered a shot from Terry Venablcs. At the other end, Peter Bonetti was reported to have performed faultlessly.

So Leicester were without silverware that year. A 1-0 defeat by Manchester United and a 1-0 home win over West Ham preceded two games with Aston Villa; at home the points were shared, but at Villa Park Aston Villa won by the only goal.

Finally the season dribbled out. On 24 April they travelled to White Hart Lane to face Tottenham Hotspur, and were beaten 6-2. Jimmy

Greaves lined up a penalty in the sixty-first minute and Gordon – without gloves – was just running his hands through the grass to clean them for a better grip. Before he knew it, the ref blew, so Jimmy kicked the ball into the net – Gordon was both astonished and annoyed, but the goal stood.

7

The Full Three Lions

Alf Ramsey's management pedigree wasn't courtesy of a top, fashionable First Division side; rather he had taken over at Ipswich Town and guided them to the championship of the Second Division in the 1961/62 season, when Gordon's Leicester were runners-up in the FA Cup to the double-winning Tottenham side. Quietly and assuredly, Ipswich took up their position in the First Division, and in their first season in the top flight they won the championship. The characteristic of that Ipswich side was that they were a team; there were no big-money signings or superstars, and sadly they were not considered an 'attractive side'. But Alf Ramsey, manager extraordinaire, had arrived. Ipswich chairman John Cobbold was a confidant of Alf, and when the England manager's job was offered he advised Alf to take it, he might not get another chance. The FA's first choice was Walter Winterbottom's assistant, Jimmy Adamson, but he had declined the job. Technically, Alf didn't become England manager until 1 May 1963, and by this date he had overseen two England defeats: 5-2 by the French team in what was then called the European Nations Cup; and a 2-1 defeat at Wembley by the Scots. He believed the defeat in Paris was all down to poor teamwork, which wasn't helped by the absence of Johnny Haynes of Fulham (England's first player to be paid £100 per week).

The defeat at Wembley by the Scots was notable for the replacement of Ron Springett in goal, by twenty-five-year-old Gordon Banks.

The last time the Scots had travelled south was some two years before when the scoreline read England nine, Scotland three! Wembley Stadium had been upgraded and now boasted an all-round roof, which took the noise level up a number of decibels! Dave Mackay returned to the Scottish team after a two-year absence, and would link up with the mighty Ian Ure in defence.

Willie Henderson impressed early on, and after a good piece of goal line running he crossed a low ball into the 18-yard box – it was a good job

Gordon's concentration was on the game and not the occasion, because Bobby Moore nearly sliced into his own net. From the clearance, Bobby Smith picked up the ball and moved out towards the right wing and away from Ian Ure. But he dribbled the ball a little too hard and Eric Caldow intercepted, the ball ran back to Ian Ure. But Eric and Bobby collided; both went down. Ian passed the ball up to Jim Baxter, but when the attack fizzled out the two players could receive help. They'd stayed down. Bobby was carried off, but Eric had broken his leg so left the field on a stretcher.

Approaching the half-hour, Willie Henderson was again active on the right wing, sending over a cross that Jimmy Armfield picked up and dribbled out of the 18-yard box. But Jim Baxter pounced and easily dispossessed him; he turned and moved towards goal, Gordon came out to narrow his angle. Jim had plenty of time to look up and pick his spot – his left foot propelled the ball to Gordon's right and into the goal.

Two minutes later, Willie Henderson was again moving in from the right wing towards goal when Ron Flowers felled him – with what Gordon later described as a tight smile, Jim Baxter converted the penalty.

Bobby Smith returned to the field, but before the referee could consent to his return to the game, Jim Baxter almost nonchalantly side-footed a ball forward, avoiding three England players, to John White who turned and struck – Gordon was equal to this and thwarted a third goal. Shortly before half-time, Bryan Douglas burst through from his own half and beat two Scots before laying the ball off to Jimmy Melia, but the ball ran loose and it was fifty-fifty who'd get there first; Bill Brown in the Scotland goal or Bobby Charlton – the former just made it.

With a half-time score of 2-0 to the Scots, it was the outfield players Alf concentrated on at his half-time talk. Gordon was doing okay, a defender error and a converted penalty had put him under unfair pressure.

Within a couple of minutes of the start of the second half, John White made a second raid through the left flank unmarked – Dave Mackay was ready for the cross, but Gordon tipped it up with his fingers so that a few seconds later he had steered the ball to safer ground and could catch it.

Willie Henderson made another of his runs down the right wing and when Gerry Byrne impeded him, Scotland were awarded a free-kick just outside of the area. Gordon was there to collect the ball with ease, but he lost it – Bobby Moore collected the ball and dribbled it out of trouble. England were gaining in confidence and composure, but each time the attack neared the Scotland goal the ball either went to high, wide or straight at the goalkeeper. The Scots' attacks were as numerous as in the first half, but they tended to peter out. From a corner Gordon got the ball but dropped it – two blue shirts tried but failed to score, and the loose ball ran to Denis Law, who still didn't make it count. The luck the Scots had was now more evenly distributed.

Bobby Charlton was a split second away from a left-footed blow, but just in the nick of time Dave Mackay tackled. But he only succeeded in pushing the ball forward to Jimmy Greaves, who shot on the turn – Bill Brown went down but the ball flew upwards and goalwards; of all people, left-winger Davie Wilson practically cleared off the line, though the ubiquitous Jim Baxter was in attendance.

England continued to attack and Gordon had less and less to do. Bobby Smith, still hobbling from his first-half collision with Eric Caldow found Bryan Douglas, and Ian Ure missed the chance to intercept, so Bryan headed for goal. His goal came nine minutes from the end.

Ian St John had received a knock and left the pitch for a while, but the nine men held England at bay until he returned. In the dying seconds, Alex Hamilton tried to find Denis Law with a high ball into the area, but the ball rolled out for a goal kick. Ten-man Scotland triumphed. Jim Baxter had been Scotland's maestro who, in Jimmy Greaves' words, was 'as smooth as silk and all style and skill'. But Gordon had made the first of many England performances and hadn't let the side down.

From a contractual view, Alf Ramsey's first game came on 8 May 1963, when of all sides it was World Champions, Brazil. In typical style, their first and only goal was a perfect example of the art of the free-kick. And it was something Alf had made a big point of to Gordon in training, and in the prematch briefing; the Brazilians were masters of directing the ball from a free-kick. For all that though, Gordon wasn't ready for just how much the ball could defy gravity, physics and all other scientific laws when propelled by a Brazilian boot. Gordon suggested the ball did 'a circular tour of the penalty area' before it entered the net, and Graham McColl suggested the flight of that ball bent to such a degree that some 'contraption – probably remote controlled … had caused the ball to do this'. Alf Ramsey was not pleased the goal was conceded and said so, again and again. Bryan Douglas was to find a way through to the Brazilian goal a few minutes before time. So against the World Champions, the game finished at one goal each.

But what starts to emerge is the camaraderie and close team spirit. Gordon had one of the best-ever left-backs in the business in Ray Wilson in front of him. Another solid defender was George Cohen, who joined up with Gordon and Ray to provide the last line of defence for many years.

The circumstances in football can be a little sad as the right-back in the next game had a career cut short by a serious knee injury, and was a superb defender – Ken Shellito teamed up with Ray to protect Gordon against a Czechoslovakian side who had lost to Brazil in the 1962 World Cup final, so the game was going to be a test – and still Alf Ramsey hadn't seen a win since taking over the job.

On 20 May, England beat the Czechoslovakians 4-2 in a game where the two goals conceded were good, but no one's fault. Jimmy Greaves got two of England's goals, which apparently so impressed the Czech players that they applauded, and Bobby Smith and Bobby Charlton the others. Alf, with Harold Shepherdson's 'club-style family spirit', was taking hold. The player's could get to know each other and talk about football, Alf had discussed his experiences as an England player, and the players looked at their teammates as friends. This helped win the World Cup in 1966.

But they were up against the East German team in Leipzig on 2 June 1963: Jimmy Armfield was in at right-back and Roger Hunt replaced the ill Jimmy Greaves. Gordon wrote that the goal he conceded was a goal he should have saved, and Graham McColl said Gordon had 'looked shaky' and the goal was 'soft'. Peter Ducke (pronounced Dook) was the German who did the deed, but Roger Hunt – in his second game for England – thumped home a shot from outside the 18-yard box, and Bobby Charlton scored the winner. The final match of the short tour was an emphatic win against the Swiss, but Gordon gave that one a miss.

Alf Ramsey had an approach to the game that players were in awe of. His preparation for a game would have him discuss the opposition in the smallest detail and his analysis would ensure his players would know what their players were likely to do! When England went to Ninian Park in Cardiff in October 1963, they almost knew what was to happen before it did, and they come away as clear winners at 4-0.

Later that month, many of the biggest stars in the world came to London to help the English celebrate the centenary of the forming of the FA. Gordon said he would have paid to play in the game as his biggest heroes were there. Lev Yashin was in goal; Ferenc Puskás, Uwe Seeler and Jim Baxter as mere substitutes. Gordon's defence held the 'Rest of the World' team at bay, but Denis Law scored with characteristic relish. Alf Ramsey was working the 4-4-2 formation far more now, and in the back four were Jimmy Armfield, Bobby Moore, Gordon Milne and Ray Wilson, who were 'ruggedly impressive'. Up front, the Tottenham partnership of Bobby Smith and Jimmy Greaves were a match for Denis Law and Eusébio. Southampton legend Terry Paine opened the scoring following up on the rebound from a Jimmy Greaves shot. After Denis Law had equalised, Bobby Charlton was soon striking towards goal and Jimmy Greaves was on hand when Milutin Soskic, the Yugoslavian second-half goalkeeper, couldn't hold Bobby's shot. The result was 2-1 in front of a capacity – in those days – crowd of 100,000.

On 20 November 1963, the Jimmy Greaves–Bobby Smith double act really sent the Wembley crowd home in warm cheer. In the first match to be played at Wembley under floodlights, the scoreline was 8-3 against Northern Ireland. Jimmy Greaves scored four goals and Terry Paine, three; Bobby Smith added the other. The three goals to sail in to Gordon's goal was to be a rare occurrence. Through his England career, Gordon kept over thirty clean sheets, and at one time seven matches were to elapse without a single goal conceded. Goals are not conceded by goalkeepers, although they're the ones who take the blame; it's a team who concede goals – Alf Ramsey was to create a defence capable of winning the highest accolade.

Gordon's own recollection of the Northern Ireland thrashing was the performance of the Northern Ireland goalkeeper Harry Gregg 'who pulled off some marvellous saves but couldn't play England on his own'. Harry Gregg was a survivor of the Munich crash a few years before, and it was he who rescued a young babe and her mother. By a sad irony it was a Manchester City goalkeeping legend who died that night, and one of Gordon's boyhood heroes – Frank Swift had taken up journalism after football and had been with the Manchester United party covering the match for the press.

In the blustery wind at Hampden Park the next April in 1964, Gordon won his eighth international cap in a single-goal defeat by Scotland. It was Alf Ramsey's tenth match in charge, and the first in which they had failed to score. Alan Gilzean headed the winner in the seventy-eighth minute when he jumped in front of Gordon – Alan seemed to know instinctively the effect of the wind and Gordon didn't, he said it was a mistake, which might be too severe a criticism. When Alan Gilzean was free in the opposition's 18-yard box area, one never knew if he would strike for goal himself or lay it off for a teammate, such was his unselfish game – it's difficult to know if he is best remembered for his 'flicks-on' and 'lay-offs' or for his striker's thirst for a goal – either way Alan's play looked so easy, which was one of the hallmarks of greatness. When a player stamps his mark of greatness on a game, it can sometimes leave his opposition looking flat-footed, which may have been more like what happened. Jimmy Greaves said Alan Gilzean was one of the greats of the game and rather than wanting all the glory himself he 'concentrates on making things happen'.

A few weeks later, England were at Wembley to play Uruguay. Jimmy Greaves came back into the side at the expense of Roger Hunt, but for the first time the two full-backs were Ray Wilson and George Cohen. Maurice Norman was still at centre-half in the heart of the defence, and Bobby Moore made up the back four. It was Bobby's first outing as captain – and it was Bobby Charlton's fiftieth cap. The game was a 2-1 victory for England, but before the match Alf Ramsey warned them that the Uruguayans were sometimes over-enthusiastic with the physical stuff, and his message was not to retaliate. In the event it was not noted as a scrappy game, though Gordon did say the strikers took a bit of stick

– Johnny Byrne scored both goals and was a lick of paint away from his third when he hit the crossbar.

But in the following match against Portugal in Lisbon, he did score a hat-trick, and Bobby Charlton also found the net. Both were lucky to be on the trip after they'd gone out on the beer with some of their teammates the night before they left London, Alf Ramsey made it clear he didn't like this, and if it persisted then those players would not be selected. Gordon suggested the night out was just a group of them 'innocently' going to a bar with a 'nice atmosphere'. It did though show Alf's professionalism – they were warned; Ken Leek wasn't.

In the event, England conceded three goals against the Portuguese with Gordon considered as 'unsteady'. He felt he did okay, but Alf felt he could have saved at least two of the goals. But the back four of George Cohen, Ray Wilson, Bobby Moore and Maurice Norman were impressive, so Alf knew he had a back four that were resilient. The back four were now sound, and perhaps would have stayed longer and jelled some more if Maurice hadn't been unlucky some while later by breaking a leg.

Gordon gave way to Tony Waiters for the next game, but that was a disaster when Ireland won in Dublin 3-1.

So Gordon was recalled for a trip to New York, and described himself as a spectator rather than a participant in England's 10-0 beating of the United States. Alf Ramsey had been on tenterhooks all through the match as he was a full-back in the 1950 World Cup finals when the United States beat England, and had never recovered from the shock and humiliation.

There was a tour and minor tournament in Brazil in the close season of 1964 that saw Brazil, England, Portugal and Argentina line-up against each other in the fiftieth anniversary of the formation of the Brazilian FA. Tony Waiters again took the goalkeeper's jersey in England's opening match against Brazil, and had the misfortune to be beaten on five occasions – three of the goals came from their classy free-kicks. Gordon was back for the next fixture, which was a 1-1 draw with Portugal – José Torres, who'd scored twice in their last meeting, was sent off for taking a swing at the ref, who he felt had been far too lenient with Maurice Norman's tackles.

It was a real eye-opener for Gordon to see just how good the Portugese and Argentinian squads were, and he was particularly impressed with the Argentine side led by Antonio Rattín. The Argentinians won the mini tournament, and it was a shame their great skills were not so evident two years later in London.

The squad went over to Northern Ireland for what was known as a Home International. By half-time, Jimmy Greaves had added a hat-trick to Fred Pickering's opening goal and it looked as though that was going to be that. But when they relaxed a bit in the second half, Gordon's hitherto perfect partnership with Maurice Norman fell apart and Northern Ireland scored three times. England were lucky to win and Alf Ramsey wasn't slow in letting them know. The other thing to create a problem for England that night but made every head turn when they saw him play was a young Belfast boy called George Best.

For the next three internationals, Tony Waiters took the No. 1 jersey from Gordon, but he returned to England duty against Scotland in April 1965. And a new debutant, at the age of thirty, was Jack Charlton – so the back four were set now in stone with Cohen, Wilson, Moore and Jack Charlton. Sadly, Ray Wilson tore some rib muscles and didn't appear for the second half. Bobby Charlton and Jimmy Greaves gave England the lead, but after a second injury – Johnny Byrne injured his knee – Denis Law pulled a goal back, and Ian St John equalised. Another debutant that day was the midfield battler Nobby Stiles, who seemed to have a favourite word: win.

In May, with Ray Wilson fit again and able to take up his left-back position, Hungary visited. The last time they'd played at Wembley was in 1953, and they'd won 6-3. The England right-back that day had made a real mess of things – his name was Alf Ramsey. So Gordon and the lads saw a smiling Alf when Jimmy Greaves scored to give them a single-goal win.

Four days later in Belgrade, Alan Ball made his debut for England in a goal apiece draw, and three days later England beat West Germany 1-0 in Nuremberg. Gordon and big Jack Charlton were magnificent, and Gordon had said he was now very familiar with the back four and his confidence was growing. Alf Ramsey now had a perfect defence. Finally on this mini tour, they beat Sweden in Gothenburg 2-1.

It was now just over twelve months before the World Cup finals in London, so Alf left the defence alone – and why shouldn't he – to concentrate on his strike force. Joe Baker of Arsenal and Alan Peacock of Middlesbrough came in and scored goals in the next match in Belfast, to see Northern Ireland off 2-1. Gordon was now comfortable at the back and had taken to thinking through his performances after the game, rather than during it.

Gordon kept a clean sheet against a Spanish side in Madrid in December, as Joe Baker and Roger Hunt scored to give us victory. Alf now had a 4-3-3 formation that was gaining momentum.

As the New Year came, England travelled away from Wembley to Goodison Park in Liverpool, where a brilliant shot on the turn by Jerzy Sadek for Poland earned them a draw – Bobby Moore scored for England.

Dress rehearsal for the World Cup final came to Wembley on 23 February, with England beating the West Germans from the single goal by

Nobby Stiles. West Ham striker Geoff Hurst made his England debut. On 2 April 1966, the England team converged on Glasgow, where a crowd of 134,000 saw Geoff Hurst score his first goal for England. Roger Hunt got two and Bobby Charlton also found the net. The England front line was now taking shape, and in early May, Martin Peters made his England debut in a 2-0 victory over Yugoslavia.

The part-timers of Finland gave England a bit of a warm-up, and Gordon noticed Alf was using many of the England squad for the World Cup, which was now only weeks away. Martin Peters seemed to dovetail so well into the 4-3-3 set-up that Gordon referred to him as 'all smoothness and style'. He kept his place for a match against a strong Poland side on 5 July, when Roger Hunt scored.

So that was the build-up for the World Cup finals in 1966, with Alf Ramsey firmly committed to Gordon Banks behind George Cohen, Ray Wilson, Bobby Moore and Jack Charlton. Nobby Stiles and Alan Ball worked like Trojans in midfield, with the elegant Martin Peters linking to Jimmy Greaves, Roger Hunt and Bobby Charlton.

8

The Countdown or
the Build Up?

Both of Leicester City's cup campaigns for the 1965/66 season were brought to an end by Manchester City. In the Football League Cup, the tie was held at Maine Road, Manchester, on 12 September, which was Gordon's first game of the season – he had broken his wrist in a pre-season friendly.

In the FA Cup, Leicester won 2-1 at Aston Villa, and by the same scoreline at Birmingham City. The Birmingham City skipper Ron Wylie summed up the game: 'There is only one reason we are not in the fifth round … the goalkeeping of Gordon Banks, we were more skilful but we just could not get the ball past Gordon when it really mattered.'

They travelled to Maine Road for the fifth round where they drew with Manchester City 2-2. The replay was at Filbert Street in March, and the headline was far from flattering; Gordon had 'fumbled a shot from left-winger Neil Young over his own goal line'. Manchester City won the Second Division championship that season.

So all Leicester could do that season was well in the League. That was not too tall an order either, as there were new signings both at the back and up front. Jackie Sinclair, a skilful winger from Dunfermline joined the line-up. Peter Rodrigues joined them later, but if Leicester were to be the quick-break specialists then they needed someone tall, fast and lean – and intelligent. They got someone with all four and more attributes; a striker who was to become one of the all-time greats in League football, Derek Dougan.

Also by now, the BBC had monopolised League football on television. Ken Wolstenholme was introducing the stars and bringing them into our living rooms. We could now see our national heroes slogging it out in the mud on a cold Saturday afternoon, and this reinforced the respect the young fans of the country had.

On 23 October, just about seven months after their last visit for the first leg of the Football League Cup final, Leicester City travelled south to Stamford Bridge to take on Chelsea in the League. It was a lovely, sunny afternoon. Chelsea were not doing too well, and Tommy Docherty decided to take a gamble and sit Barry Bridges on the substitutes bench and bring a young eighteen-year-old centre-forward into the team to make his debut – his name was Peter Osgood.

It was that big figure of Derek Dougan, towering above Jimmy Goodfellow and Davie Gibson, who kicked off for Leicester. Chelsea were quite unlucky in their first attack, Joe Fascione linked up with Jim McCalliog, and Jim was able to take the ball to the goal line before hitting it back to Joe, whose effort went right across the face of the goal with Gordon stranded at the near post. Terry Venables was on the far side but his attempt to get the ball back over was in vein, but Chelsea won a corner.

At the other end, Derek Dougan got a lucky rebound but Peter Bonetti held well. Peter Osgood won the ball and sent Joe Fascione off, but he seemed to overrun the ball, though he did manage to keep it in play – he centred but John Sjoberg used little effort to clear easily.

By half-time there was no score.

At the start of the second half, Peter Osgood sent Bert Murray charging into the Leicester City 18-yard box, but he lost his balance at the critical moment. Leicester started to have a bit more fire in their attack. Jackie Sinclair teed the ball up for Mike Stringfellow on his left foot, but it hit the post and there was a bit of a scramble before the ball went out for a corner. John Sjoberg, up from the back, positioned himself perfectly and arrived to head the ball from the 6-yard line into the corner of the net to Peter Bonetti's left.

Chelsea did not sit back. John Boyle pumped in a long cross that Gordon got a hand to and when it fell it was quickly booted upfield. Ken Shellito felled Bobby Roberts just outside the 18-yard box, and although the kick produced little, it did show that Leicester were enjoying more control. But in the last line of defence, Peter Bonetti was showing his class. At the other end, Ken was active, and he pounded a free-kick high and long that, again, Gordon only got a hand to before Bobby Roberts could boot the ball out, only to be played back in.

A lightning break by Leicester was countered by an equally quick break by Chelsea, and Peter Osgood, taking a pass from Terry Venables, looked dangerous – on the edge of the 18-yard box his right-footed shot was pushed out by Gordon.

Bert Murray for Chelsea floated a ball in, and Gordon was off his line like a shot to deny Tony Fascione. After a quick throw out, Peter Bonetti was very soon out to deny Derek Dougan a scoring chance. Tony Fascione ghosted into the 18-yard box and turned on a sixpence to clip an up and under that Gordon just managed to get a hand to for a corner.

Bert Murray took the ball from the flank to the centre of the pitch, and from just about 25 yards he put in a fierce shot that was deflected and lost some of its power – but a deflection means any preparatory work the goalkeeper might have done has to be quickly reassessed: Gordon dived to his right and made a magnificent save.

Bobby Roberts took the ball up for Leicester and shot, but the shot was again deflected away from Peter Bonetti and straight into Derek Dougan's path – luck went against Peter. So at 2-0, things looked good for Leicester. Jackie Sinclair hit the post and when the clearance went upfield Barry Bridges (on as substitute for Eddie McCreadie) was chasing, Gordon came way off his line, and like a centre-half he headed the ball away.

Final score: Chelsea nil, Leicester City two.

Three weeks and two wins – Arsenal at home, and Everton away – later they faced a Manchester United side at Filbert Street. Gordon described the season of 1965/66 as 'topsy-turvy' and in this encounter, if Matt Gillies' maths was reliable, Leicester City had thirty-four corners; the result is something that will come out shortly. For Manchester United that afternoon was David Herd, of whom Bobby Charlton said had the hardest shot that he knew of in football. Manchester United played in an all-white strip, which brought the black-and-white viewer some relief, as with Leicester in blue the teams would have been indistinguishable. Shortly after the kick-off, Gordon dived to his right, completely missed his objective and the entire ground erupted in a cheer; he failed to catch a dog that wanted to exercise on the pitch. Eventually the canine was sent off and the match continued.

But Gordon was like the invisible man. Even though I've only seen highlights, the game during the first twenty minutes or so was almost entirely in Manchester United's half. That changed a bit with a good Manchester United move and a good methodical build-up. Finally, David Herd was almost to the goal line when he pulled it back for John Connelly to side-foot it home. Against the pressure, Manchester United took the lead.

Gordon was seen more now, and he did have to move a bit quickly for a Graham Cross back pass that could have been an own goal, but luck was with him – briefly. Leicester had three shots charged down in as many seconds, but could not find the net. Gordon made a good save from a Bobby Charlton long-range strike, and managed to retrieve the ball before Denis Law poached. On thirty minutes, David Herd gave a display of his shooting power. George Best laid the ball across to him and David was at slow pace, but when he hit the ball he was almost stationary. Gordon dived to his right but could not get to it, so Manchester United were now two goals up. Interestingly, Bobby Charlton said later that he thought shooting against Gordon from outside of the 18-yard box was a 'pointless exercise' because Gordon always saved them.

About a minute from half-time, David Herd was there again. George Best centred and David was completely unmarked, and with a header he could pick his spot. Just as half-time was upon them, Harry Gregg made a good save from a Bobby Roberts strike.

At half-time Manchester United were three up.

Leicester started the second half on the attack, but it seemed the ball was going to do anything for them except go in the net. At the other end, Gordon dived well to his left to save a shot from George Best.

Graham Cross hit the post and Ken Wolstenholme said it just was not going to be Leicester's day. Bobby Charlton broke through and hammered in goal number four. George Best picked up a pass in his own half and as the attack developed, David Herd was in position, but his effort went wide. A few minutes later, George was on the ball again as he nonchalantly dribbled in to make the final score 5-0.

The following Saturday at St James' Park, the score was Newcastle United one, Leicester City five. Topsy-turvy was right. In December after a 2-0 defeat by Nottingham Forest, they saw Sheffield Wednesday off 4-1. They lost 4-2 at Burnley before it was their turn to score five goals at Filbert Street against Fulham – the only serious threat to Gordon was a long-range shot from England teammate George Cohen that he palmed onto the post before retrieving the ball close to the goal line.

Finally, as April brought a bit of green back to the trees, Leicester were guests at Old Trafford, but this time they won. They were hosts to Newcastle United but lost, before they won 4-0 at Fulham. For the hosts, Steve Earl got behind the defence and sent a ball across, which Gordon managed to cut out. He saved well from Les Barrett and then a quick break saw Fulham goalkeeper Jack McClelland kick the ball away in what was more of a tackle on Jackie Sinclair. Gordon saved with a 'fantastic reaction' from Graham Leggat just before half-time. Derek Dougan headed in a Jackie Sinclair cross for 1-0, and Tom Sweenie set up Jackie for Leicester's second goal. A penalty was awarded to Fulham, and Bobby Robson strode up to take it. Gordon managed to push it over the bar; 'Banks underlined his brilliant form with a fine save.' Derek Dougan and Richie Norman scored the other two Leicester City goals.

Four days later, they travelled across the Midlands to West Bromwich Albion, where Jeff Astle demolished them. Poor old John Sjoberg scored twice for West Brom, the first was a Jeff Astle strike that John had tried to cut out, and the second was just a few moments from time. John Kaye scored twice, and Jeff Astle also netted; Jeff had set up all the West Brom goals.

'Gordon Banks did not handle the ball with his usual safeness.'

Leicester City finished a decent seventh in the First Division that year, despite their roller-coaster ride of results; they won twenty-one games, drew seven, and lost fourteen. Gordon appeared in thirty-seven fixtures, of which five were cup ties – he managed to keep a clean sheet for ten of those games. On the last day of the season, West Ham with Bobby Moore, Martin Peters and Geoff Hurst were all intent on beating Gordon. They did not, but Geoff centred for John 'Budgie' Byrne to head in the winner.

Just in time for the World Cup, Roger Hunt was leading scorer in the First Division with thirty goals, though some were in cup competitions. With only a few months left, England as hosts automatically qualified for the World Cup finals – as did Brazil as champions.

The 1965/66 season was when the last final whistle was heard on a Christmas Day.

9

Before it was All Over

It looked like it was Bobby Charlton who took the first kick of the 1966 World Cup finals in London. He, Roger Hunt and Jimmy Greaves all stood over the ball waiting for the whistle, and then, suddenly, the ball was in play and the tournament had started – a tournament Alf Ramsey said England would win. They looked unlikely to lose their opening match; with the back four in front of Gordon, the Bank of England might have been easier to get into than the goal of Banks of England! But could they win it? The match was played on a warm, sunny Monday evening at Wembley, in front of 87,148 spectators.

John Connelly formed the front three with Jimmy Greaves and Roger Hunt, and it was important for England not to lose the game or concede any silly goals. The match ended in a goalless draw, and despite what people have said down through the years, this was okay.

In the first few minutes Uruguay looked a bit nervous in defence but soon settled – they played with four at the back and then another between those four and the goalkeeper. One move fairly early on opened up the England defence, and even though it finished in an offside, it showed the Uruguayans were a force. England were tidy at the back and could break quickly.

Gordon was seen from time to time, but his concentration was quite clear. Uruguay strung a few passes together and they were patient, when they had the ball they liked to slow things down. The patience was nearly rewarded when Julio Cortez struck the ball from a good 25 yards that Gordon could only parry, so a corner.

There were a number of infringements for obstruction in the game, which demonstrates how the game in South America differed from the European game. From one free-kick Bobby Charlton had a sight of goal, but his finish was about a foot over the bar.

The tight defence of the visitors and England not wanting to concede any goals made the game a little tedious.

Half-time: 0-0.

The second half did not promise anything more appetising. There was the threat the match would deteriorate following a high challenge against Bobby Charlton, but things settled again. Bobby Moore marshalled his defence and when Pedro Rocha burst through, Bobby was there. One could be forgiven for thinking that Gordon was having a night off because there had only been one real occasion where he had acted against a shot. Crosses did not seem to occur.

The Uruguayans' goalkeeper, the twenty-one-year-old Ladislao Mazurkiewicz, was well protected, but when he was called on he did not disappoint. But a couple of England attacks typified the Uruguayans – Nobby Stiles ventured into the 18-yard box picking up an Alan Ball pass, but three defenders appeared from nowhere. Similarly, Alan Ball led an attack and three defenders were on him all at once. Their play was good solid defending and breaking when possible, they were a good side.

But as the second half progressed so did the excitement. Pedro Rocha provided a bit of inspiration when, with his back to goal, he flicked the ball up, turned and struck first time, a good move but all that resulted was a goal kick.

An England attack of some promise started but at the end of it, Ladislao Mazurkiewicz was equal to it. Bobby Charlton on his left foot shot from the edge of the 18-yard box, it was heading through a crowd of players and threatening to go just inside the left post, but a good save.

Alan Ball worked harder and harder as the game progressed, and even took on five of the Uruguayan defenders and passed to Roger Hunt. Nobby Stiles was up in attack and finally a ball went off goalwards from an English head – not very accurately but still goalwards. Jimmy Greaves took up the ball outside the 18-yard box on the right. Moving in, he crossed and John Connelly was just thwarted – one touch would have been a goal. And still Alan Ball worked hard and George Cohen had made some overlapping runs – usually at great speed. One cross found Jack Charlton, who headed back across the goal for John Connelly to head it up to just clip the bar. But the whistle had gone. Jack then got up to a Jimmy Greaves cross and he headed back across the face of the goal, but this time John Connelly was just off balance and could not connect. Uruguay were lucky.

Final score: 0-0.

After the final whistle, Alf Ramsey said he had been happy with the performance, but not with the result. At least Gordon got some goal-kicking practice in, but no small point to make; Gordon was the only goalkeeper in all the groups to keep a clean sheet in the group stages. I know I have made much of the back four and they were equally praiseworthy. But the striking efficiency must have worried Alf. For the second game he brought in Terry

Paine of Southampton as an out-and-out winger, and Martin Peters to midfield. Considering that Alan Ball had worked so hard in midfield and John Connelly had two of the best goalscoring chances, it seems as though Alf was still considering his strike force.

The group was effectively left on level pegging after the second game between France and Mexico. This game finished in a 1-1 draw, so England were not disadvantaged by a draw in their opening game. On the Friday night, France were in action again when they were beaten 2-1 by Uruguay, which gave the South American's an advantage on points and a good advantage psychologically. As host nation, England were under pressure and nothing short of a win, preferably by a couple of goals without conceding, would best suit in their next game.

And they did not disappoint. But the Mexican team on the Saturday night fixture did defend with consummate skill. Salvadore Reyes kicked off for Mexico, and his teammate Isidoro Díaz booted the ball upfield straight to Gordon. One wonders about the thinking behind this! For the first five or ten minutes, the signs were that England were going all out for a win. Terry Paine floated in a free-kick that Jack Charlton nearly connected with and Roger Hunt narrowly missed. Jack would be making the excursion up quite regularly and Bobby Moore spent a good bit of time in the opposition's half.

It was not until the fifteen-minute mark that Gordon was called on to keep goal rather than just take back passes. Mexico did show a little danger on the quick counter-attack and they began to settle.

Bobby Charlton got in a cross that Jimmy Greaves just missed out on; and a few minutes later Bobby Moore became a stand-in centre-forward and nearly scored – this was from a George Cohen cross, so the back four were defiantly looking for trouble. Roger Hunt found the net – Bobby Charlton had crossed to the far post and Martin Peters had nodded the ball back, but he was offside.

It looked like Martin Peters who intercepted a pass and the interception found Roger Hunt, who laid it off to Bobby Charlton just about at the rear end of the England half of the centre circle. Bobby moved forward and just over seven seconds later it crossed the goal line at terrific speed after Bobby had propelled it with his right boot. One of the best goals of the tournament after a superb run – Ken Wolstenholme thought he was about 35 yards out when he struck it. That was what England needed.

Just before half-time a Mexican attack saw Gordon take the ball off a Mexican head for a corner. Roger Hunt met a cross surrounded by three Mexican players and their goalkeeper.

Half-time: 1-0.

When the second half started, most of the early play was in the Mexican half of the field; England took control. But they weren't going to have it all their own way; Gordon punched the ball off a player's head in one early attack.

Martin Peters connected with a George Cohen cross, but the ball went over and landed on top of the net. Gordon and his back four were having few problems with the Mexican attack.

Bobby Charlton won possession, laid off and received back; laid off and received back and into the Mexican half; a through ball to Jimmy Greaves, who took the ball through a couple of defenders and turned. His shot from a diagonal angle with his left foot was not held by Ignacio Calderón in the Mexican goal, and Roger Hunt was there to just sidestep the ball over the line. England two, Mexico nil.

About five minutes from time Gordon dived at the feet of Enrique Borja, but there was no real danger – and Gordon's only touch after this was for a goal kick.

Final score: England two, Mexico nil.

The press said the result was 'unconvincing' and the performance was 'competent' and England did not really look like candidates for glory – but Alf, Gordon, Bobby Moore and everyone else had different ideas.

Gordon was not conceding any goals so the other goalkeepers in the squad – Ron Springett and Peter Bonetti – were unlikely to play. The next match with France again showed no change in the back four; they only needed a draw against France. It's interesting that the first two games of the tournament were against South American sides that were rich in football skills but came to defend, whereas the third was against a European side that were willing to play in a more balanced style. Later a word can be said about the Argentinians who *could* play good football against the home nation, though much happened on the blind side of the referee, but a European side who played rough against a South American side – Brazil's Pelé was hacked and fouled until he had to withdraw from the finals!

So for the final match in group one, England lined up against France at Wembley Stadium on Wednesday 20 July. The orthodox right-winger Terry Paine was replaced by more of a left-sided midfielder in Ian Callaghan, and Martin Peters continued in his midfield role. As the game progressed, one could once again identify George Cohen being a right-back when the match demanded but a high-flying right-wing attacker when the game allowed. Similarly on the left with Ray Wilson. Gordon had Bobby Moore and Jack Charlton in central defence, and he was quite happy with this. A win was the aim, and if Gordon could continue to keep a clean sheet against the best footballing nations in the world, then so much the better.

France kicked off, but after just a few minutes trainer Harold Shepherdson was on tending to an injured Nobby Stiles – he collided with the referee!

Ten minutes or so into the game and France got a corner; Gordon needed to punch the ball from a converging forward who got a little too close to the goal line for comfort. So again, England were not going to have it all their own way. Gérard Hausser collected the ball and was allowed to within 10 yards of the England 18-yard box without challenge – he made a good chip for Robert Herbin's head in a good move that resulted in a goal kick. France were playing attractive football.

England made some good moves, but with Robert Herbin limping one could not help but think this placed the French at a disadvantage. Gordon and Jack Charlton had a bit of a misunderstanding when Jack made a pass back, but it went out for a corner. Gordon let Jack know he was not too pleased with the incident, but from the corner came another corner and the attack fizzled out.

Ian Callaghan nearly placed a shot/cross in the net, Marcel Arbour in the French goal managed to push the ball over.

Bernard Bosquier tried a long shot, but Gordon had little trouble. There was little problem for Jimmy Greaves to find the net at the other end, but the ref found his whistle and offside was the conclusion to rule out Jimmy's effort.

Just before half-time, Bobby Charlton let go with one of his thunderbolts that Marcel Arbour did well to save. From the corner the ball was sent back out to Jimmy Greaves, who clipped it into the far post where Jack Charlton was in acres of space, but he headed it against the post – Roger Hunt was there for the rebound for England's first goal.

Half-time: England one, France nil.

The second half started well enough, but without too many goal area incidents. Just on the hour, Gordon made a great save. France broke from an England attack and after some good first-touch pinpoint passing, Bernard Bosquier played in a cross from a position closer to the halfway line than the 18-yard box. The ball was bending on an arc towards Gordon's goal and Jacques Simon connected superbly to target the ball to the bottom corner – Gordon dived to his left and just prevented the equaliser.

Bobby Charlton nearly put England two up but was ruled offside. This did not affect the French composure, but a second goal was looking likely. Again Bobby won the ball in midfield and made his way out onto the left wing; his cross went right across the area for Ian Callaghan to pick up, and his cross found Roger Hunt arriving just ahead of Martin Peters. Roger's header found the top corner of the net and England were two goals up.

Sadly, Jacques Simon had gone down during the action, and once the goal had been scored and play temporarily stopped, he could get some help. He was carried off the field, which took France down to ten men and Robert Herbin had been hobbling for a good while. Jacques came back on a few minutes later but could not participate fully.

It looked like England had the game sown up and would be at the top of the group. Philippe Gondet hit in a fierce shot after a slow build-up by the French. Gordon dived to his left again to make a good save. But the final score was 2-0 and England topped their group. They had five points from the three games and Uruguay, who won one match and drew two, were second in the group.

Gordon later gave lots of little insights in his writing. For instance, in his 1980 *Banks of England*, he describes Nobby Stiles as a fair but hard competitor. He also describes how Alf Ramsey supported him and kept the critics at a distance. But Gordon also unwittingly exposes a paradox: Portugal gave England their toughest but most entertaining game, Argentina their toughest and hardest. No serious injuries were recorded in the England Argentina game, but the Portuguese defenders did injure a player; in their fixture with Brazil at Goodison Park, Pelé was hacked down and injured for the next game. There were as many fouls or infringements by the England players against Argentina as the Argentinians committed – though it did not seem as though their captain, Antonio Rattín, was sent off against England as a direct result of this or for bad play.

It was on Saturday 23 July that England faced Argentina in the quarter-finals. As the game was about to start, Ken Wolstenholme commented on Antonio Rattín and said he was one of the 'greatest players in the world'.

Luis Artime got the match underway, and it started in what could be called a vibrant manner. It was to be a physical game and not one of the class one would have liked from the two teams.

Alan Ball was flattened in the penalty area by an Argentinian tackle, but the referee ruled 'play on'. Geoff Hurst rose to meet a Ray Wilson cross, and was crudely body checked – not a foul in those days, but he was knocked flying. However, England committed as may infringements as their opponents. A deceptive cross played in by Oscar Más would have caught out a lesser goalkeeper, but Gordon managed to collect the ball just about a yard from his line. And he punched out a free-kick that was swerving in towards his goal. Oscar Más led the attack again, and when he shot for goal he produced a good save from Gordon, who proceeded to collide with the post.

But then Jorge Solari was cautioned and miles away from play and the ball, their captain Antonio Rattín was sent off. This seemed a bit strange as it was reported this was for 'violence of the tongue' and Rudolf Kreitlein, the referee, was quoted to have said he did not speak Spanish. The game was held up for a good few minutes and Ken Aston, who was in a supervisory role for the referees, intervened. I'm not sure if Mr Rattín's pleas of bewilderment were completely bogus, and on watching the game numerous times England were as 'hard' as Argentina. It was a shame Alf Ramsey and the word 'animals' were linked up, as Gordon has since said the reporting of it was not wholly accurate. But Alf did stop George Cohen swapping shirts with an Argentinian player.

Ken Wolstenholme commented, 'They've never seen anything like this for a long time.'

The match limped and dived and walked towards half-time – what happened isn't really worth discussing.

Bobby Charlton set the second half in motion, but there was little excitement; Bobby Moore had a dubious handball awarded against him, and George Cohen hacked Oscar Más down – this gave Argentina a free-kick and when it went high into the 18-yard box, Gordon could punch clear.

Ray Wilson sent over a cross that Geoff Hurst could chest down, and with two defenders between him and the goal, he turned and shot, which produced a good save from Antonio Roma in the Argentinian goal. Jack Charlton collided with Antonio when the ensuing corner came over. At the other end, Jack was the perfect answer to high crosses, shielding Gordon.

Twenty minutes into the second half and Oscar Más was heading towards the England goal, Gordon came out to narrow the angle and he may have come too far. It gave Oscar the opportunity to place the ball, but when he did the ball was wide and England survived. Argentina slowed the game right down. Jimmy Hill was in the commentary box with Ken Wolstenholme and commented that England needed to get men down the flanks and to the goal line, and that's how they would score. And that is just what they did. At eighty minutes, Geoff Hurst got away from his marker and met Martin Peters' cross perfectly for England to take a 1-0 lead. Gordon even came up the field to join in the celebrations. This was the 100th goal they had scored under the management of Alf Ramsey.

From the kick-off a long shot nearly caught England napping, but Gordon had not lost his concentration. Argentina then found out just how good England were at protecting their goal and lead.

Final score: England one, Argentina nil.

Gordon said later that there were off-the-ball incidents like spitting and the odd sly punch from the Argentinians. And the war-like attitude continued after the final whistle when four of them came into England's changing room looking for a fight!

It seems as though Antonio Rattín was sent off for dissent at questioning or criticising the referee's decisions. Gordon was to say that Herr Kreitlein should 'shoulder some of the blame'. He felt the official had punished minor infringements, but serious misdemeanours seemed to go unpunished. The president of the Argentinian FA, although he made a point of saying he disapproved of some of the players' tactics, roundly criticised Herr Kreitlein. Most commentators, including Gordon himself, have said that if Argentina had played to their abilities that day, then they would really have given England a run for their money.

As the pantomime was played out with Antonio Rattín, Ray Wilson and Gordon noticed the score from Goodison Park was Portugal nil, North Korea three. Now that was noteworthy. But the Portuguese star striker then hit form, scoring four goals out of Portugal's five to win – though there was probably quite some stress in the Portuguese camp that afternoon.

So all was set for the semi-finals, and Portugal, who were the leading scorers on fourteen goals, were to take on England, who were yet to concede a goal in the entire competition. Alf Ramsey made no change to the team that had knocked out Argentina, and Ray Wilson gained his fiftieth cap.

England got the game underway. After a few minutes, Bobby Charlton sent a long ball through the defence that Roger Hunt chased. José Pereira, the Portuguese goalkeeper, was soon off his line and managed to get there first but miskicked his clearance, however the danger passed.

José sent a long-kicked clearance upfield that bounced three or four times and into the hands of Gordon. He too sent a long ball out, Roger Hunt controlled it to Geoff Hurst who teed it up for Bobby Charlton, but his shot went straight to the goalkeeper.

Gordon was not troubled at all in the match until a low cross came in from the right as Jaime Graça joined in the attack, but the legs of Jack Charlton took it out and Ray Wilson was on hand to shield Gordon as he collected the ball.

Nobby Stiles headed a ball out for a corner – he had to because Eusébio was coming in behind him. When the corner was taken, Eusébio sent an in-swinging cross, but the ball went out for a goal kick.

Alan Ball sent in a cross that found the Portuguese defence a bit one-footed, but so was the England attack. Fortunately, José Pereira was up to speed; but he had it and lost it – the ball rolled across to Geoff Hurst whose shot produced a good save from the quickly recovering goalkeeper.

Full-back Alberto Festa crossed, the ball fell to António Simões, who controlled the ball and turned before shooting from the corner of the 18-yard box – Gordon was equal to the shot.

The Portuguese attacks were exciting, but as ever the England back four were outstanding. José Torres was a tall striker and powerful in the air, so the crosses were looking for him, but he was not always best positioned. England were finding their forwards, a Geoff Hurst shot lacked power but, again, it was on target.

Eusébio was very nearly on target with a 25-yard ground shot that Gordon just got a hand to – so a corner. This time José Torres met it but could not make it count, Jack Charlton harassed him all the way. After a brief bit of play around the England 18-yard box, Bobby Charlton took the ball out and sent it well upfield.

Tommy Docherty had joined Ken Wolstenholme in commentating and he felt after about half an hour that the game needed a goal, but suggested that it did not look as though either team would score. Ray Wilson from deep in his own half almost put the ball onto Bobby Charlton's boot on the edge of the Portuguese 18-yard box, the ball then found Roger Hunt, who dummied José Carlos by going one side of him while the ball went the other – this took half a second and José Pereira managed to send the ball out of Roger's control. But lurking on the edge of the 18-yard box was Bobby Charlton, who side-footed the ball over the goal line to put England ahead.

About two minutes later Bobby was on target again, as was Martin Peters a few minutes after that – José Pereira had been perfectly positioned for both.

At the England end, José Torres was active but again the ball did not go goalwards. He was still there a few minutes later for the next cross, but did not connect. The ball ran loose to Eusébio, who kicked it perfectly with the outside of his right foot and it was on target; Gordon dived to his right and for the second time denied Eusébio. The skill was even but the luck was going England's way.

A few minutes later, José Torres got the ball controlled and his right-footed shot sizzled past Gordon's left post. Eusébio came down the left flank with George Cohen and Alan Ball in tow, but managed to get a corner. José Torres did manage to get on the end of it and headed back across the goal into Gordon's arms.

Mário Coluna shot from the edge of the 18-yard box, but again Gordon saved. The back four were effective, but so was the Portuguese attack. In the England attack, Martin Peters sent in a cross and Roger Hunt just failed to connect.

As the teams went off at half-time the score was 1-0 to England. By far the best display of skill, tenacity and sportsmanship of the tournament so far.

Shortly after the restart England won a corner, and when Jack Charlton came up for it, José Torres came with him. A few minutes later, Jack was in his own half denying José any luck; Jack at full stretch to give Portugal a corner. Gordon punched the corner clear.

Alberto Festa took a long shot, but Gordon was able to take it with the minimum of trouble. A Portuguese free-kick went hopelessly wide, and a few minutes later a cross towards José Torres found Jack Charlton.

A free-kick was given to Portugal to the right of the 18-yard box, therefore Gordon's left, but when the ball approached goal he punched it clear again. He had said that his first training session at Chesterfield had been on a punching bag and he asserted that these skills came in handy later – there were a good few examples in this game.

Bobby Moore had an uncharacteristic lapse in concentration and gave away a free-kick. Seconds later José Torres won the ball in the air. It then went onto Eusébio's head and goalward. Gordon terminated this attack with consummate ease.

Portugal kept up the pressure, but the only thing they seemed to need was luck – a shot on goal lacked power and went straight to Gordon.

Halfway through the second half, Bobby Charlton got into a shooting position but was just off target.

It was as though Portugal could easily get the ball into a dangerous place but there was no one there to finish.

George Cohen sent a long ball downfield. Geoff Hurst chased and won the ball inside the 18-yard box, though a bit too close to the goal line. He had time to look up and around and even though by the time he controlled the ball a shot may have been possible, he almost casually rolled the ball back to where Bobby Charlton was converging, right boot at the ready. It was one of the best moves of a match full of good moves, and even the Portuguese players congratulated the scorer of the second goal. At 2-0 there was one of the best sights of the tournament, Jack Charlton congratulating his brother.

It was ten minutes from time when Portugal kicked off, and they'd dismissed any acknowledgement of the word 'beaten'. António Simões chipped in for José Torres, who headed back across the goal; for once Gordon seemed beaten and so did Jack who handled to avert a goal. And so a penalty. Gordon had considered this eventuality and knew where Eusébio might want to put it, but communications in the Portuguese camp, and more frantic communication in the English camp, decided where Eusébio might shoot, so that was Gordon's best option.

But the outcome was a goal and Eusébio collected the ball to take back towards the centre circle, giving Gordon his acknowledgement as he did. Eusébio gave Bobby Charlton the ball. It was the fiftieth goal against England since Alf Ramsey had taken charge, and the twenty-seventh goal Gordon had conceded, and all England could do now was hang on. But they were not a team to defend as a matter of course, though Portugal came out with a determination difficult to describe.

Geoff Hurst was sent galloping forwards, and managed to get into the 18-yard box. He laid the ball off to Bobby Charlton but it was not to be a repeat of the earlier spectacular strike, and the ball was passed back to José Pereira.

The next attack saw Portugal's José Torres send the ball vaguely goalwards, but the attack fizzled out. A few seconds later, a long ball upfield found José Torres again and his header found António Simões in acres of space, unmarked and about 10 yards from goal. Gordon was out like a rocket to narrow his angle, but again luck was not with the Portuguese; António could not control the ball sufficiently to strike with force.

With two minutes to go a high ball went into the English 18-yard box, Gordon was off his line and up to collect. At the other end, Bobby Charlton put in a left-footed shot, but José Pereira was perfectly positioned.

With just about a minute to go, Mário Coluna put in a fierce shot that Gordon managed to just tip over the bar. That was one important save.

The final score was England two, Portugal one. England were in the final to meet West Germany who had beaten USSR by the same scoreline.

Gordon later described that semi-final as *the* classic football match.

One interesting observation is that Jack Charlton was at the centre of defence that evening and gave the match his all. Nobby Stiles though, was actually singled out by Alf Ramsey as making the most outstanding contribution because he managed to contain Eusébio. Watching the game again one can see Alf's point, but that match was won with indescribable style.

West Germany had beaten Cyprus and Sweden to qualify. Then in England they started the final campaign with a 5-0 win over Switzerland at Hillsborough that was followed by a goalless draw with Argentina at Villa Park. They secured their place in the quarter-finals by beating Spain 2-1, again at Villa Park on 21 July. They then returned to Hillsborough, where they destroyed the tight Uruguayan defence with four goals and conceded none. After this it was across to Liverpool, and at Goodison Park they took to the field against Lev Yashin's USSR. The result was 2-1, so West Germany were the first of the countries to book their place in the Wembley final.

England had scored only seven goals to reach the final; Germany thirteen. And in defence, England had conceded Eusébio's penalty in the semis, West Germany had only conceded two goals. So both attacks were adequate and both defences were polished.

Despite pressure on Alf, England were unchanged from their semi-final match, which meant Jimmy Greaves, who had taken a knock in the final group match against France, was sidelined, and Geoff Hurst continued in attack alongside Roger Hunt. The Germans brought Horst-Dieter Höttges back into defence, who had been replaced by Friedel Lutz for the semi-finals.

One of the high points of Gordon's autobiography is the description of the England changing room in the final few minutes before going out onto the pitch for the final. The things that were going through his mind – would he need gloves? His preference was always gooey and sticky hands as this helped better grip the ball. But as it rained he decided to take globes along too, just in case. And then off they went, Gordon chewing gum like it was going out of fashion – he took gloves as well because the rain had made an appearance, so it was impossible to decide if gloves or bare hands smeared with gooey saliva, courtesy of the chewing gum, were best.

Siggi Held set the ball in motion and the 1966 World Cup final had started. Hans Tilkowski in the German goal got a touch in before Gordon when he took a goal kick. Gordon got his first touch when he placed the ball down, again for a goal kick after Siggi Held was just off target.

Both sides settled well and after about ten minutes, Nobby Stiles was up with the attack. He centred and up went Roger Hunt with Hans Tilkowski, who got there with his fist. But he could only punch the ball out as far as Bobby Charlton, who had time to turn and centre again. Hans was up again, this time with Geoff Hurst, but as the two collided, the ball came out and the whistle went as play had gone on with an infringement.

Jack Charlton set Martin Peters in motion, who shot from the corner of the 18-yard box, but Hans Tilkowski made a good save.

Karl-Heinz Schnellinger passed the ball first time to Siggi Held, who sent over a long, high ball. Ray Wilson misunderstood the instructions from his fellow defenders who wanted the ball left so it would go into touch. His header was not powerful and it fell to Helmut Haller, who controlled it with his right foot and turned towards goal. Bobby Moore was over to him as quick as lightning, but just before he could tackle Helmut shot with his right foot. Jack Charlton was just in front of Gordon but an inch or two away from being able to make an effective clearance, and Gordon diving to his right just could not get a hand to the ball.

1-0 to West Germany.

So a rare mistake at the back. Ray said later that as one of the older of the players, he could soon put it behind him to concentrate on the game. The main thing was now to just knuckle down to it. Wembley, for all its glory, was the worst place to be on a losing side – Gordon had experienced that. As if sensing this, Bobby Moore was to rally his side. About six minutes later, he made a rather uncharacteristic excursion upfield. But just about midway from the centre line and the corner of the 18-yard box, Wolfgang Overath intercepted and felled Bobby. Time for something special: Bobby took up the ball and placed it on the Wembley turf all ready for the free-kick ... he knew what he wanted to do, and so did his West Ham United teammate, Geoff Hurst. Before anyone on the field, or even in the crowd, could draw breath, Bobby's right foot sent the ball towards Hans Tilkowski's goal. As it dropped just about level with the penalty spot, it met Geoff's head about a yard from the 6-yard line. There were four defenders all spaced at about 6 yards from him – to both sides and to his front and rear; Hans stayed on the goal line. Geoff met the ball perfectly and the five German players could only watch as the ball hit the netting to equalise.

Had this happened at the other end, Gordon and his four main defenders would have been as powerless against such a set piece.

From a West German free-kick of Karl-Heinz Schnellinger to the far post, both Ray Wilson and Bobby Moore were up to defend, but they were beaten in the air by West Germany's Uwe Seeler, whose timing of jumps was perfection – fortunately Gordon was there to collect. Uwe repeated the feat a few minutes later.

Bobby Charlton managed to get away from Franz Beckenbauer for half a second for a left-footed shot that Hans Tilkowski saved comfortably. But a minute or two later, Franz got away from Bobby and sent Uwe Seeler away to pass forward to Helmut Haller, but Gordon got to the ball a fraction of a second quicker.

About ten minutes or so before half-time, George Cohen placed a perfect high ball on to Geoff Hurst's head, just about level with the penalty spot. Two defenders were with him but his header to Hans Tilkowski's right nearly crept in, so a good save, Alan Ball was there, but by the time he could put the ball back in, five or six German players were in attendance.

Siggi Held received the ball from Franz Beckenbauer and entered the 18-yard box accompanied by George Cohen. Nobby Stiles took possession of the ball and fed Alan Ball. He passed it back to George, who was momentarily off balance, but Siggi Held was not. George recovered though his options weren't great, but a sliding tackle from Jack Charlton sent the ball out for a corner.

Siggi Held sent over the corner. Bobby Moore got a foot to it, but it only went as far as Wolfgang Overath who hit it first time with his left foot. Gordon dived to his right, made a good save but did not hold it – it fell to Lothar Emmerich, whose left foot shot past a quickly converging George Cohen and Martin Peters, and was caught by Gordon.

Alan Ball and George Cohen were active in the corner of the pitch and finally got the ball out to Bobby Charlton; Roger Hunt was on the end of his cross, but Hans Tilkowski was there to make a good save. A few moments later and Bobby again put Roger through, but Wolfgang Weber was there for the Germans.

Siggi Held, leading the counter-attack, passed to Uwe Seeler at the halfway line. Uwe shot from about 35 yards and it was dipping under the bar before Gordon made another good save.

At half-time the score was one goal each.

Rain fell as the second half started, and England were determined to keep play in the German half of the pitch. But a good break ended in offside.

The game got into what Ken Wolstenholme described as a 'midfield stalemate'. Gordon made the odd save but there was nothing particularly to tax him. He punched out a Helmut Haller cross, and a few minutes later Siggi Held beat defender after defender to win a corner. The English back four were looking quite comfortable. Jack Charlton came up for a free-kick and almost changed the course of history.

Things brightened up in the last twenty minutes or so, and Billy Wright who knew the Wembley pitch as well as anyone said that in the last twenty minutes, the pitch might give England an advantage.

Alan Ball won a corner on the right, which he took. The ball went over a good few heads and fell to Geoff Hurst, who shot with his right foot; the ball cannoned off Horst-Dieter Höttges and fell perfectly for Martin Peters' right foot. It was not a perfectly elegant effort, but it became the most important shot of his life; it hit the back of the net with a huge roar. It was twelve minutes from time.

Soon after the restart, Karl-Heinz Schnellinger almost got a free effort from the corner of the 18-yard box, but it went straight to Gordon. From a free-kick Wolfgang Weber got in a header but was wide. Bobby Moore signalled to his players to calm down. About a minute from time, Wolfgang Overath got in a shot but was just wide.

Jack Charlton beat Siggi Held and headed clear of danger, but the referee said it was a foul; so a free-kick. Lothar Emmerich blasted the free-kick into the wall and on towards goal. George Cohen connected but it fell to Siggi Held, who shot with his left foot; the ball hit Karl-Heinz Schnellinger, and Gordon suggested there was a handball. Bobby Moore appealed and he was the other side of Karl-Heinz with a better view. The fact is if the ball hadn't hit him it would have shot across the face of the goal with some speed. When the ball hit Karl-Heinz, the power was taken out of Siggi Held's strike, so Uwe Seeler would not have connected and Wolfgang Weber would have been too late. But it looks as though the ball hit Karl-Heinz on the area immediate above and between his side and the middle of his back – his flailing arms do not help to pinpoint quite where, and watching video at normal speed it does look doubtful. In the event, Uwe Seeler could not quite connect but Wolfgang Weber could, and did: 2-2. Seconds after the restart, the referee blew for the end of ninety minutes.

In the break before extra time, the England players looked dejected – it was the first time that extra time had been played in the final. But off they went.

Alan Ball had a very good run that finished with a right-footed drive, and Hans Tilkowski pulled off a good save. Jack Charlton on the left wing gave Geoff Hurst a perfect centre, but the ball was deflected and went for a corner. The move finished with a Bobby Charlton effort that hit the post. Roger Hunt was just off target a minute or two later.

Nobby Stiles sent a long pass to Alan Ball, who just about caught up with it by the corner flag; he played it first time. And there was Geoff Hurst, perfectly positioned with time to control the ball with his right foot before turning and striking from just about 7 yards. The ball hit the bar and bounced down to the ground. Roger Hunt, who had the best view in the stadium, said the ball had gone over the line, so he turned away in celebration. Was it a goal? The referee ran over to consult the linesman. It was a goal.

By half-time in extra time there was no more excitement, just twenty-two exhausted men watched by several million who all must have wondered where Alan Ball got his energy from. As the second period of extra time got underway, passes went astray but the standard of competition never diminished.

Roger Hunt shot just inches wide of the left post. The pace slowed (apart from Alan Ball). With about a minute left to play, Germany got a corner – Gordon was able to punch it away. Back went the ball for Bobby Moore to chest down and pass out, only for it to be passed straight back to a now in-space captain. He looked up and saw Geoff Hurst, who knew it was not all over, as did Wolfgang Overath, who nearly caught up with him. This time it was his left foot.

I'm still not sure if there was actually a kick-off after this, though Gordon told me there was, the BBC and ITV television cameras were more focused on England having done the possible, not the impossible. Gordon was to ask later, as the team were celebrating with the rest of the squad before going up to the royal box, 'How did we feel at this particular moment?' The answers from the other players doing a commentary for the DVD:

'Shattered!'

'Fantastic.'

Geoff Hurst said he felt relieved to have got through it.

Gordon said, 'To think that you'd won it though. That was a great feeling.'

He mentioned to the others that the goalkeeper would end up mentally drained after the match. But it was, 'a great day – super, super day'.

But there was a news story that meant England nearly did not get presented with the World Cup, and could have died of embarrassment. Prior to the competition starting, the Jules Rimet Trophy was on display with a stamp collection at the Methodist Hall in Westminster; it was in a locked cabinet and a security firm were employed. But it went missing, although the lid turned up at Mr John (Joe) Mears' home through the post. He was the chairman of the FA at the time, and was strongly linked to Chelsea. The lid of the trophy was accompanied by a note of extortion for £15,000. The cup was found, however, by a dog called Pickles in Upper Norwood. A Edward Betchley was later jailed for sending the note and was cleared of being an accomplice to the thief. It appears that the thief was never identified.

But England did win it and Her Majesty the Queen presented the trophy to Bobby Moore. Every mortal soul of England will remember that day. Some will remember the emotion of Bobby Charlton, the slip of Jack just after he collected his medal – one of the few times he ever lost his footing. Most will remember Nobby Stiles skipping in football boots as majestically as Gene Kelly had danced in roller skates.

There is still controversy over the last-minute free-kick though, and about Geoff Hurst's second goal, and the arguments might rage but will never effectively be concluded. Jack said he did not foul Siggi Held but the referee said he did – so he did. Germany equalised. The German team to a man said the strike from Geoff Hurst hit the underside of the crossbar and bounced out without crossing the line. The referee said it did cross the line – so it did. All the teams who entered that tournament, and indeed any team that kicks a ball throughout the world, agree to abide by the rules of the game – and the rules are clear that the referee has the final say. We can look at Jack Charlton's challenge over Siggi Held and say perhaps it was a bit harsh to penalise – whether there was a handball in the goalmouth scramble that ensued is another debate. The fact was Wolfgang Weber slid the ball into the net and the match finished two goals each. But nearly fifty years on, the discussion over Geoff Hurst's first extra-time goal looks set to go on for another fifty years!

What can't be taken away from England is that the two goals they conceded were unfortunate, and two of the goals that England scored were hardly world-class. But two of goals they scored that afternoon were. When Geoff Hurst danced into the area without a German player near him to finish off a perfect set-piece from Bobby Moore's free-kick – that was world-class. Gordon said it was pure Ron Greenwood from West Ham and not Alf Ramsey; but it was Bobby Moore's vision and Geoff Hurst's anticipation. And the other world-class England goal? Was this the final kick in the 1966 World Cup finals?

Academic now, but after the German equaliser: from the kick-off until the ref blew for time at ninety minutes, there was a total of five seconds of football played: Bobby Charlton side-footed to Geoff Hurst who passed back to Jack Charlton – before he could play the ball; before the ball had actually left the centre circle, the referee blew for the end of ninety minutes. When the Germans kicked off at 120 minutes – if they kicked off – then the match was almost immediately over: based on the commentary by Ken Wolstenholme it was about eight seconds – which meant the ball from the West German kick-off might have gone out of the centre circle. The videos and so on I have seen of the match show nothing more after Alan Ball congratulates Geoff Hurst on his third goal – so the last kick in the 1966 World Cup finals and who made it is a question I leave unanswered. It would have been a bitter blow to the Germans if Geoff's second goal was the deciding strike, so thank fate there was a fourth goal and that was superb football. Can I say then that if I can't identify who made the last kick in the tournament, could one settle for the last kick that mattered? But in this I have a dilemma, most folk would say it was Geoff Hurst, but is it possible to suggest that with the desperate German attack and the way the ball was calmly played out of defence into attack by Bobby Moore then that was the last kick that mattered – yes, it secured a fourth goal for England but as importantly it denied a further attack on Gordon's goal.

So for the first time England were world champions. Thinking about the entire squad, and Alf Ramsey and Harold Shepherdson, the feeling is best summed up by Gordon Banks: 'We had brought so much joy to so many people.' Not half.

10

The England Goalkeeper's Jersey

Alf Ramsey – or Sir Alf – was the only England manager Gordon played under at full international level. The manner of a manager is to keep enthusiasm going, therefore the player would never be quite sure of his place; Sir Alf certainly had this philosophy. He even asked Gordon how he felt when he was not selected for the team; the message Gordon gave was he wanted to occupy that jersey and would do all he could to do so. That's what Sir Alf wanted.

I have looked at Gordon's international career up to and including the World Cup finals of 1966, and the way one might normally set out a career would be, perhaps, his journey to the top, his time at the top and the emergence of younger players. But in Gordon's case, he got to the top and was improving! Gordon was a pioneer of the concept of the goalkeeping coach, and built up the expertise as his career evolved. Even though Peter Shilton seemed to be Sir Alf's first choice of goalkeeper after Gordon's accident, I do not think it coincidence that the immediate successor as England goalkeeper was later a first-class goalkeeping coach, that being Ray Clemence.

I'll discuss the Mexico World Cup in 1970 a little later, but the reason England did not win the World Cup in 1970 was because we were beaten by West Germany in the quarter-finals. West Germany were then beaten by Italy who were then annihilated by Brazil. West Germany struggled to beat us and it was more stamina and luck – and more luck. Brazil struggled too, and in the build-up to their winning goal the referee should have given England a free-kick because Tostão elbowed Alan Ball in the face – but most commentators of the 1970 finals would say that when England were playing, the referee did not seem to see all that he might! My point is that England were more than a match for the eventual champions. Of course it's impossible to say that if Brazil hadn't scored England might still have done so a few minutes later when the fresh Jeff

Astle, on as a substitute for Francis Lee, just could not quite connect when he had a good goalscoring chance. But then rewinding to the first half, Francis Lee had a superb effort saved by Félix in the Brazilian goal. In 1970, Gordon was still looking at ways to improve his game, and was experienced as well as physically and mentally on top: 'I hit the pinnacle of my career … and felt so confident in everything … I know I could not have been in better form than I was in Mexico in 1970.'

From the last game in the 1966 finals – which was the final – to the opening game for England against Romania in Mexico, Gordon kept goal for England for twenty of the twenty-six matches played, which is over three times the amount of games by the other three top-class goalkeepers we had – Peter Bonetti, Alex Stepney and Gordon West – put together. So there can be no doubt that Sir Alf thought Gordon was at his best too. I'll discuss his club exploits throughout this period a little later, but in 1967 Matt Gillies and the Leicester City board thought football had seen the best of Gordon. But there were plenty of people around who did not take that view, including Tony Waddington, the manager of Stoke City.

But thinking about his England career, Gordon was with the other ten from the World Cup final when they visited Windsor Park in Belfast for a tie with Northern Ireland in late October 1966. UEFA had conceded that the season's home internationals could also be the qualifying group for the European Nations Cup – now called the European Championships. England won 2-0, with Roger Hunt and Martin Peters on target. On duty for Northern Ireland, there were the iconic figures of George Best and Derek Dougan, and if anyone were likely to score it would have been either or both. Most of the veterans from the 1966 final will say that on the international scene, England were the team everyone wanted to beat.

The World Cup finals had seen an increase in televised football, and *Match of the Day* was now well established, not quite with the technology of today but good enough to be getting on with. Gates were up too.

In early November 1966, the eleven played together at Wembley for the first time since the World Cup final. Gordon describes the opponents, Czechoslovakia, as forming a nine-man 'blanket defence', and Gordon said he had to fight with himself to keep his concentration as most of the game was played in Czechoslovakia's half. He said that without a high level of concentration on the game, quick breaks can catch out the best. The match finished as a goalless draw, and Sir Alf was perhaps disappointed for the 75,000 or so who had turned up, as was Gordon, but Sir Alf's midfield were now his pride. But England could stop goals, score goals and had the most dynamic midfield, so it was only a matter of time before the Wembley crowd were again to see a superb display.

They did not have long to wait. A fortnight later over 70,000 had crammed into Wembley for a match – the second of the European

Championship qualifiers – against Wales. Ken Wolstenholme said there were many more spectators still arriving at Wembley, where he described road and pedestrian routes as being 'chock-a-block'.

Bobby Charlton got things underway, but very little of note happened in the first half-hour; Gordon took a couple of back passes and perhaps a goal kick or two. Geoff Hurst opened the scoring for England when his 35-yard crack got a deflection past Tony Millington in the Welsh goal. Geoff added another quite soon after when he headed home a Nobby Stiles cross.

Gordon had to retrieve the ball from his net just before half-time when Wyn Davies got between George Cohen and Bobby Moore; he dived to his right but Wyn's header was the perfect compliment to a Ronnie Rees cross.

Three minutes from half-time, Bobby Charlton produced his usual magic with his right foot to make the score at half-time England three, Wales one.

Wales opened the second half with an attack, but when Cliff Jones headed towards Gordon's goal, he could collect the ball quite easily. That was not the case during the next Welsh attack because Ron Davies's shot from the edge of the 18-yard box actually beat Gordon, but it was the post that denied him.

The luck got worse for the Welsh because when poor Terry Hennessey lashed out at a Roger Hunt strike, the ball went up and over Tony Millington and under the bar for an own goal. Jack Charlton was on the end of a superb cross from Geoff Hurst to make the score 5-1.

About five minutes from time, the combined efforts of Ron Davies, Wyn Davies and Mike England managed to get the better of Gordon for a cross from a corner, but the ball went out for a goal kick.

The match was not over though, and a huge roar echoed around Wembley when Ronnie Rees lifted the ball into the England 18-yard box and Gordon fumbled it, quite harmlessly, and he passed it out to George Cohen. Ken Wolstenholme summed it up: 'That was very un-Gordon Banks-like. Wasn't it?'

The final score was England five, Wales one.

April 1967 was when England took on Scotland at Wembley; it was the final match together for the formidable back four of George Cohen, Ray Wilson, Bobby Moore and Jack Charlton. Bobby Moore was a mainstay, and the other three continued in international shirts from time to time.

The rivalry between England and Scotland made any fixture between them one which both wanted to win, and the atmosphere was taken up a good notch or two when England had become world champions – and so it was the Scots made the journey south from Largs in mid-April 1967. In their run up to the World Cup, England had beaten the Scots by 4-3 at Hampden Park in Glasgow the previous April.

The only change from the World Cup-winning side was Jimmy Greaves coming back to replace Roger Hunt. At Wembley that afternoon, the noise was deafening.

Scotland kicked off. Gordon's first touch was a back pass, which did not really excite the crowd. Tommy Gemmell sent over a cross; no one was there for Scotland, but the determination and support was clear.

Jimmy Greaves sent over a corner that bounced off the bar for a goal kick. With only about a quarter of an hour gone, Jack Charlton hobbled off, and as there were no substitutes in those days England had to soldier on with only ten men. It transpired Jack had broken his toe, but he did eventually return to the game.

A good move by the Scots started when Denis Law dispossessed George Cohen and it came to its climax through Eddie McCreadie sending over a centre Bobby Lennox tried to get on the end of, but Gordon was there to take the ball.

Bobby Charlton made a great run but was just beginning to lose his balance when his shot from his right foot went goalwards, but it was just over. A free-kick to Scotland just outside the 18-yard box saw John Greig blast it just wide. Gordon took a short goal kick out to Bobby Moore who then passed back to Gordon, but the kick was not strong and Willie Wallace got there first and dispossessed Gordon. He sent over a centre Denis Law received in front of an open goal, but his effort hit the side netting. Scotland should have taken the lead then.

Jim Baxter got his head to a corner, but Gordon was there ready to take possession. From a free-kick, Eddie McCreadie gave the ball to Jim Baxter who took it towards the England goal, passed to Willie Wallace who played a one-two with Jim before shooting from the edge of the 18-yard box. Gordon was down to save well but he could not hold it – in went Denis Law and Scotland took the lead.

England's passing was not great, but every time England got possession there was a Scot wanting it back.

Willie Wallace put in a shot/cross that Gordon took quite easily but the fact was the ball got through the England defence – they were missing Jack Charlton at the back as he had taken up more of a forward position. That nearly paid off soon after when Nobby Stiles crossed and he met the ball unmarked and got in a good header – but Ronnie Simpson in the Scottish goal made a good save.

Jim McCalliog was not going to give up possession, and retrieved his ball to pass to Jim Baxter. He took it goalwards and found Billy Bremner, who passed first time into Denis Law's path – Gordon was off his line fast and the two collided. The game went on up to the opposite penalty area for Ronnie Simpson to kick the ball into touch so his opposite number and Denis Law could receive some attention. The game was soon restarted.

Just before half-time, Bobby Lennox got in a shot that took a deflection for a corner, but the score at half-time was England nil, Scotland one.

Billy Bremner shot wide a few minutes after the restart. England did not really look any sharper than they did at the end of the first half. Bobby Lennox picked up the ball just inside the English half and managed to travel to within a hair's breadth of the goal line – he could and should have been challenged, but he centred low towards Denis Law. Gordon was there to clear up.

A few minutes later, Alan Ball did a similar thing for England before a low centre to Martin Peters to strike and Jimmy Greaves to follow up, if Ronnie Simpson hadn't got there first.

Tommy Gemmell put one just past the post for Scotland, and Willie Wallace soon got a chance to shoot, but it hit the side netting.

Scotland attacked again and Ray Wilson could not stop Bobby Lennox, but the ball ran lose to Bobby Moore who passed back to Gordon. The Scots were sharp and kept possession, and soon regained it if they lost it. Billy Bremner took the ball into the 18-yard box, but Nobby Stiles and Gordon merged to stop his progress. Willie Wallace shot weakly and Bobby Lennox hit the side netting again, but was offside.

Scotland cleared a Jack Charlton effort off the line through John Greig. England were fighting. They were unlucky when Martin Peters put in a shot and Geoff Hurst managed to follow up, but Scotland were off the hook through Ronnie Simpson's fine save.

Tommy Gemmell blasted one that ricocheted high, and his follow-up header eventually found Bobby Lennox, who turned and shot. That made it 2-0.

Gordon took a Willie Wallace corner comfortably. And it should be remembered that Jack Charlton was still on the pitch in a hobbling forward position. Alan Ball passed to Jimmy Greaves who back-heeled to Alan to pass to Jack, who finally found the net for England.

The minutes were ticking by and with the score 2-1 in Scotland's favour, there was a piece of Gordon Banks action that is easily on a par with the save against Pelé – but this was really quite different. Denis Law received the ball and moved towards the 18-yard box, from a yard or so outside he chipped the ball high and goalward. By the time the ball left Denis's foot, Gordon was a good way off his line and was about midway between the 6-yard box and the penalty spot. The ball travelled up and when it reached its peak height, Gordon was just turning to head back towards goal. As the ball fell, Gordon completed his turn and timed a leap to perfection to palm the ball out for a corner. On freeze frame he appears horizontal and about 6 feet above the ground when he took his swipe at the ball. He landed, rolled and got up to prepare for the corner.

A few seconds later, Gordon stopped another strike from Denis Law. Billy Bremner took the ball up and found Jim McCalliog, who found Willie Wallace. Jim ran on and was in a perfect position to take a return ball, and on his right foot he guided it past Gordon's near post – he said later he should have had that covered, but the move was fast and furious.

Geoff Hurst got his head to a Bobby Charlton cross/shot and made the score 3-2. And that was the final score, with a hard-fought battle and sharp, decisive finishing, it had been a terrific game. Billy Wright was in the commentary box with Hugh Johns, and he said it was the 'best game of football between these two sides I have seen for a very long time'.

It was clear that Sir Alf could not rest on his laurels. Peter Bonetti made a couple of appearances in the England goalkeeper's jersey against Spain and Austria in May 1967, but Gordon was back for meetings with Wales, Northern Ireland and the USSR later that year.

Gordon was on duty again in an unusual mid-season clash with Scotland that resulted in one goal each. He was there again in April for the quarter-final of the European Nations cup, but was said to be 'unfit' for the second leg – Peter Bonetti kept goal.

Manchester United's Alex Stepney stood in for a clash with Sweden, but Gordon was back against West Germany and the semi-final defeat in the European Nations Cup in June – he was also there for the third-place play-off. In November, Gordon kept goal against Romania, but Gordon West helped England secure a draw against Bulgaria just over a month later.

Gordon was beaten twice in three games in early 1969 against Romania and France, and even though Northern Ireland were defeated 3-1 in May, Sir Alf said, 'We'll have to do better than this.' Gordon West was in goal against Wales four days later, but Gordon returned for a 'superb match' against Scotland.

The England team toured Mexico, Uruguay and Brazil after the 1968/69 domestic season had ended. On the last day of May 1969, Sir Alf helped Gordon onto a plane home before the first game as his father had passed on. It's a measure of Sir Alf's nature that, when he broke the news to Gordon, a flight with a car to meet him at the airport on both sides of the Atlantic had been arranged. Gordon West was with the squad and stepped in against Mexico, which resulted in a goalless draw. Coming back for the funeral (as well as being perfectly professional and gentlemanly) meant a 12,000-mile round trip, with flights of about twelve hours each way, in addition to the journeys to and from the airports. But he made it back and was refreshed to play against Uruguay on 8 June. Gordon enjoyed this game and, after the few days, it seemed to focus him back onto his football. He had been close to his dad but his upbringing

1. Chesterfield youth team at Old Trafford. (*Copyright Chesterfield FC Community Trust Heritage Project with especial thanks Stuart Basson*)

2. Chesterfield youth team, runners-up in FA Youth. (*Copyright Chesterfield FC Community Trust Heritage Project with especial thanks Stuart Basson*)

3. Chesterfield first team, August 1958. (*Copyright Chesterfield FC Community Trust Heritage Project with especial thanks Stuart Basson*)

Above: 4. Peter Wright scores for Colchester United. Peter was to score the first-ever League goal against Gordon Banks. (*Copyright Colchester FC with sincere thanks to Matt Hudson and Lindsey Wright*)

Left: 5. February 1961. The all-conquering Tottenham Hotspur beaten at home by Leicester City. Terry Dyson is thwarted by Gordon Banks. (*Copyright Getty Images*)

6. England debut, April 1963. Gordon with Maurice Norman (No. 5) behind him and Scotland's Ian St John. Dave Mackay looks on. (*Copyright Getty Images*)

7. July 1966, England were to beat France 2-0. Here Gordon walks out followed by Liverpool's Ian Callaghan. (*Copyright Press Association*)

8. Gordon with Jeff Astle taking the field for the final group match in Mexico against Czechoslovakia. (*Copyright Mirrorpix*)

9. Gordon taking the ball with ease against Pelé, Mexico 1970. (*Copyright Mirrorpix*)

Above: 10. Great, Greater and Greatest! Referee Roger Kirkpatrick (*centre*) with Peter Bonetti and Gordon Banks, 1970. (*Copyright Getty Images*)

Right: 11. Gordon leads Stoke City onto Hillsborough's pitch for FA Cup semi-final against Arsenal in March 1971. (*Copyright Getty Images*)

12. Stoke City 2, Chelsea 1, March 1972. Peter Osgood shoots along the floor to equalise for Chelsea. (*Copyright Getty Images*)

13. Gordon Banks applauded onto the pitch for a fixture with Everton in 1972. He had just been named Footballer of the Year.

14. Just a few weeks after the accident, Gordon talks to the press. Billy Wright, looking on, was in broadcasting with Midlands Television. (*Copyright Mirrorpix*)

15. Helmut Haller holding a cup – but not the World Cup. Gordon is on far left with Martin Peters and Bobby Moore is behind Helmut along with Hans Tilkowski and Geoff Hurst. RIP Helmut and Bobby. (*Copyright Press Association*)

Above: 16. Hero in 2012
as Gordon Banks carries
the torch for the London
Olympics. (*Copyright Press
Association*)

Left: 17. Gordon Banks
in Birmingham, 2013.
(*Copyright Jim Morris*)

would have told him to arise – 'dust down and back t'mill'. On his mind was the experience he needed to play at that altitude, ready for the 1970 World Cup finals.

The Uruguay tie saw Francis Lee score the first goal for England to lead 1-0 at half-time. In the second half, Juan Martin Mujica sent a free-kick into the 18-yard box that Luis Alberto Cubilla managed to get his head to in full flight. Gordon was beaten and did get a hand to the ball – later he was to criticise himself for leaving his dive too late by a fraction of a second. Geoff Hurst was kind enough to get the winner ten minutes from time.

And then Brazil. Would England finally beat the best in the world? Well things started very promisingly when Colin Bell scored a goal after fourteen minutes – and this gives me a good opportunity to look at two goalkeepers dealing with almost identical goals.

To give him his full name, Gilmar dos Santos Neves was voted the best Brazilian goalkeeper of the twentieth century, but he doesn't even appear on the IFFHS (International Federation of Football History and Statistics listings for goalkeeper of the century – Gordon was second).

To look then at the two goals. Back in 1966, Wolfgang Weber was about level with Gordon's near post, about 4 yards from goal and played the ball with his right foot as he collapsed onto his left. (There was a slight difference in camera angle/height.) Colin was about level with Gilmar's near post, about 4 yards from goal and played the ball with his right foot as he collapsed onto his left. On both, the power of the shot was not really a factor; they were both almost certain to score and they were almost identical strikes. The difference is with the goalkeeper. For Gilmar in the Brazilian goal there was no other player within 2 yards of play. When Colin strikes the ball, Gilmar is roughly halfway to his near post, and when the ball hits the back netting he is just about at the near post – he had stayed on the goal line. When Wolfgang strikes the ball, Gordon had the complication of Ray Wilson flailing limbs just about everywhere, which is what he is expected to do, but it does impede Gordon's view. Gordon, in the meantime, is about a yard off his line and is behind Ray (could he see through him? Plenty of people would think so!) and starts to dive to his left, and as the ball strikes the netting he is at his near post. So both were goals, but as the ball crossed the goal line, Gilmar is at least two feet away from the ball and Gordon missed the ball by what looks like two inches. So with his lightning reactions, Gilmar just failed to save. With Gordon it seemed as though, not only could he assess the situation with a player impeding his view, but he had accelerated lightning reactions! Also Gilmar was on his goal line, and Gordon about a yard out – this demonstrates Gordon had a fraction of a second less. That would seem to be the difference between a great goalkeeper and a master of his art.

Gérson was tackled by Brian Labone and a penalty was given. Up struts Carlos Alberto, who can do just about anything with a ball – until he faces Gordon Banks. Gordon dived to his right and made a save – he later said he double bluffed him, but with all due apologies to the future Brazilian captain, he did not hit it as hard as he could.

Tostão hooked the ball past Gordon's right to equalise in front of the 135,000 crowd (in *Banks of England*, Gordon mentions '160,000 screaming, yelling Brazilians', which was a simple mistake because the match commentator sounded like a crowd of 25,000.) Two minutes later, up pops Jairzinho. Tostão takes the ball down the right wing to the goal line, and beating a full-back into the bargain, centres for Jairzinho to pick his spot high in the goal to Gordon's right, who just failed to stop the shot diving to his right and rearward.

But as it was, England lost 2-1.

For the last two internationals of the 1960s, Peter Bonetti was capped – against Holland and Portugal – and he kept clean sheets.

In January 1970, a Dutch side came to England and Gordon kept goal, which he also did for the next nine games into the 1970 World Cup finals in Mexico. From those ten games there was only one defeat, against Brazil in the searing heat of Guadalajara. Peter Bonetti stepped in when Gordon was unwell for the quarter-final tie against West Germany, and the entire 1970 tournament, with its drama and heartbreaks, is something worth a closer look later.

The other Peter, Peter Shilton, took the field against East Germany in November 1970.

By 1971, it seems that Peter Shilton was the regular understudy to Gordon, and played for his country against Wales in the home international, and against Switzerland in the European Championship. Gordon played twice against Malta and Greece, and then against Northern Ireland, Scotland and Switzerland. Peter was capped twice and conceded two goals; Gordon was capped seven times and only conceded two goals. Four goals conceded in nine games reflects on the defensive line-up too, and when considering Sir Alf capped ten different defenders during those nine games, it reflects on the skills of the defenders emerging. Roy McFarland of Derby County was most capped, but that was only in six of the fixtures.

The England team were to go on tour in South Eastern Europe in the summer of 1972, but the players were exhausted after a long domestic season and the tour was cancelled. Their last fixture of 1972 (a goal to nil win against Wales in Cardiff) came after Gordon's accident, so I'll just have a quick look at the other fixtures that year.

Gordon donned the goalkeeper's jersey for four of the six matches. At Wembley in April, West Germany won 3-1 in the European Championship quarter-final, though England managed to hold them to a goalless draw a fortnight later in Berlin. In a two-week period in May, the home internationals saw England beat Wales in Cardiff but suffer a 1-0 defeat to Northern Ireland at Wembley. Gordon was on duty for the last time in an England jersey in Glasgow on 27 May 1972. The only other survivors from the 1966 final were Bobby Moore and Alan Ball. It was Alan who scored the goal to give England a 1-0 win, seemingly catching Bobby Clark with his legs in the wrong position. Gordon said it was a fitting (if premature) end, and who better to defeat. His arch-enemy Denis Law was in a Scotland jersey, but with Bobby Moore and Roy McFarland so solid in defence it was only Asa Hartford who penetrated – Emlyn Hughes cleared off the line.

So Bobby Moore – Sir Alf Ramsey's envoy on the pitch – and Sir Alf himself on the touchline were both there for Gordon's seventy-third cap, as they had been for his first.

Peter Shilton wore the jersey in early October for England's draw with Yugoslavia; he had been on duty too in May for the fixture at Wembley with Northern Ireland. Peter is the most capped player for England, but I am quite sure if there hadn't been an accident that October, or if Gordon had recovered and retained his full vision, then history would have read differently. Peter Shilton was a great goalkeeper, but his own description of Gordon goes even further than this, perhaps as far as its possible to go: 'He's the best in the world.'

11

From Leicester City up to Stoke City

Gordon and Leicester City kicked off the 1966/67 season with an unsuccessful attempt to take points from Liverpool at Anfield – Liverpool won 3-2. A good scoring match, but the World Cup win was to lead to the turnstiles scoring hand over fist. Attendances were up everywhere and, if the summer had seen cup fever, then the autumn of 1966 was to see attendances shoot up like the temperature in flu.

A trip up to Blackpool secured Leicester's first point of the season in a 1-1 draw. Gordon was the 'outstanding player of the match'. Bobby Waddell came close to scoring for Blackpool early on – a 40-yard drive was just tipped over the bar – and in the last minute he put in a powerful drive; sandwiched between these two saves was his goal for Blackpool. Ray Charnley and John Green also brought out good saves from Gordon. Jimmy Goodfellow equalised for Leicester.

Derek Dougan said he wondered after Leicester's next game that, if Leicester had the best goalkeeper in the country, then what would have been the score if they had the worst. They let in four goals to a visiting West Ham, but West Ham let in five! Gordon said he was not too worried at the scoreline, provided his team scored more than the opposition. With Derek, Jackie Sinclair got a hat-trick, and Jimmy Goodfellow helped. Peter Brabrook and Geoff Hurst scored two apiece for West Ham.

Leicester took both points from Blackpool at Filbert Street on 30 August, and then shared the points with Sheffield Wednesday at Hillsborough three days later.

A Tuesday night fixture at Stamford Bridge saw Gordon well beaten in the eighth minute by Peter Osgood. Charlie Cooke then dribbled around him to make it 2-0. A minute before half-time, Derek Dougan headed in a Richie Norman cross. In the second half, both Chelsea's goalscorers nearly added when they hit the post, and Peter Bonetti made a good save from Derek Dougan. Gordon made a save from John Hollins with a twisting leap described as 'sheer brilliance and beauty'. Davie Gibson equalised for Leicester and Peter Bonetti made a couple of 'Banks-like saves'.

September saw Leicester City score seventeen goals in total while only conceding six. They beat Reading 5-0 in the Football League Cup, and in the First Division they scored twice as many goals as their opposition. Apart from Liverpool on the opening day of the season, they were on an unbeaten run. Come October they travelled down to London and met Arsenal.

Arsenal had just signed George Graham from Chelsea and Colin Addison from Nottingham Forest, and both scored on their debut. But the luck was not going to last – Terry Neill limped off, and Frank McLintock took time out for four stitches. Leicester made a mockery of their defence, and the final score was Arsenal two, Leicester City four.

They beat Lincoln City 5-0 in the Football League Cup, and then saw off Nottingham Forest. On 15 October, they travelled up to Burnley and in the pouring rain took on Ralph Coates *et al.* and lost 5-2. But even though he was beaten five times, he saved 'brilliantly' from Gordon Harris, and Ralph Coates and dived bravely at Andy Lockhead's feet; a little later the two were up, and Gordon literally took the ball off Andy's head. When Gordon Harris scored, Gordon was unsighted. Andy Lochhead headed in off the post; Willie Irvine headed in a Ralph Coates cross. Jackie Sinclair pulled one back just after the break, and Ralph knocked in a shot Gordon had parried. Alex Elder – later to team up with Gordon – lobbed in number five, and Derek Dougan made the final score 5-2.

In the latter part of October, Leicester travelled down to Loftus Road to take on Queens Park Rangers in the Football League Cup. At that time they were sixth in the First Division, and Rangers were in the Third Division. A total of 20,735 packed the ground – the highest crowd for years to see mighty Leicester beaten 4-2. Les Allen shone for the Rangers that night, and few sides would have survived them in that form. Matt Gillies said, 'Rangers deserved to win ... I was very impressed.'

By half-time, Derek Dougan had scored twice for Leicester and Roger Morgan had replied, but after the break there was nothing stopping them. Les Allen chipped up and over Gordon, and the ball bounced in off him for the equaliser. Les then scored with a 20-yard drive, and Mark Lazarus finished off. Queens Park Rangers went on to win the Football League Cup that season.

A trip up to Leeds saw Johnny Giles score twice and Jimmy Greenhoff once, Derek Dougan's replied for Leicester to make the score 3-1. In mid-November on duty for England, Gordon injured his shoulder so missed Leicester's next game against West Bromwich Albion. He was fit for the visit of Manchester United on the last day of November – at the time top of the League. Denis Law opened the scoring with a 25-yard drive that bounced awkwardly, and George Best made it 2-0 just after half-time. Davie Gibson scored for Leicester just before time.

In the run up to Christmas, they beat Stoke City at Filbert Street 4-2 but lost away to Tottenham Hotspur. Over Christmas and New Year, they lost twice to Fulham – Graham Leggat scored a hat-trick in the later fixture at Craven Cottage – but they beat West Ham United at Upton Park. Gordon said of the West Ham fixture, 'I have had some bad performances since the World Cup and some good ones. This was one of the good ones.' It was said that the game essentially came down to a duel between Gordon and Geoff Hurst, who said, 'Gordon was in great form.' Peter Rodrigues twice cleared off the line for Leicester.

They were at home to Sheffield Wednesday on the first Saturday of 1967, where Gordon thought his opposite number Ron Springett in the Wednesday goal effectively won the match for the visitors: 'It was Ron's good display that gave them the points'. Leicester had all the play in the second half but just could not score. The only goal of the game came after nine minutes when Gordon's future teammate at Stoke, John Ritchie, found the net for Wednesday.

They had a 4-4 draw at Southampton in mid-January 1967. Ron Davies scored a hat-trick in the first half, Tom Sweenie replied before Martin Chivers put the Saints 4-1 up. Davie Gibson, Tom Sweenie and Bobby Roberts squared the account. Southampton's goalkeeping debutant, Gerry Gurr, made what Gordon described as a 'brilliant' save from Jackie Sinclair's penalty.

They beat Liverpool at home with Mike Stringfellow and Graham Cross doing the honours, and poor Peter Rodrigues putting through his own net. A crowd of 32,049 saw the incident. They also saw Tommy Smith intervene to make sure Gordon and Ian St John did not come to blows in the last minute!

Sunderland took both points at Filbert Street. A trip up to Maine Road in the FA Cup saw Manchester City beat them 2-1, even though Tom Sweenie scored after two minutes. Gordon saved twice from David Connor, and then from Colin Bell – both looked sure goals. Graham Cross and Bobby Roberts headed off the line towards the end of the first half. Gordon managed to push Stan Horne's strike onto the bar only for Glyn Pardoe to score. Mike Doyle secured Manchester City's win.

So they were out of both cups, and the League championship had long ebbed away. In February, they won away at Aston Villa and at home to Arsenal. They lost at Nottingham Forest and drew at Everton, before a 5-2 defeat at the hands of Manchester United.

Two months after their FA Cup exit they travelled up to Maine Road, and even though Colin Bell caused a lot of stress to the Leicester defence,

Jackie Sinclair scored twice to Ralph Brand's response from Manchester City.

Tottenham Hotspur took points away from Filbert Street, and Manchester City took none. Newcastle won by the odd goal, and a 0-0 home draw with Leeds meant Gordon had played his last for Leicester City.

On 17 April 1967, he joined Stoke City for £52,000. Peter Shilton had wanted first-team football, but there may have been far more to it than that. The usually astute Matt Gillies telling Gordon his best years had passed would become one of the clangers of the 1960s. Tony Waddington later called the signing of Gordon the bargain of the century.

Stoke City was originally formed as Stoke Ramblers in 1863; they moved to their home of The Victoria Ground in 1878. Notts County are the only professional side still in business from when Stoke City formed. They were founder members of the Football League, and when Stoke became a city in the 1920s, they renamed themselves Stoke City.

In 1930, Stanley Matthews played for Stoke for the first time, and he remained in first-class football until he was fifty, so had a career spanning thirty-five years. Tony Waddington served the club for half as long, but brought Stanley back to The Victoria Ground a few years before its present president joined the club – Gordon Banks.

Gordon's debut for Stoke was at Stamford Bridge on Saturday 22 April 1967, and Chelsea goalkeeper Peter Bonetti said, 'Banks is the greatest.' Gordon dived right to stop a Tommy Baldwin shot, and left to deny Peter Houseman. When John Hollins blasted a shot, his arms seemed to lengthen to push the ball around the post. Tommy Baldwin scored the only goal.

Leicester City came to The Victoria Ground in Stoke to be beaten 3-1!

A defeat by Arsenal and a no-score draw in Gordon's second visit to Old Trafford that season rounded the 1966/67 season off.

Mr and Mrs Banks got themselves a new house. Robert, who was now nine, and Wendy, around four, were to get themselves new schools and the whole thing seemed to go off without a hitch. He had been happy, he said, at Leicester, although the pay had been a bit of a bone of contention, but at Stoke he seemed to settle in quickly and he describes the Stoke atmosphere as one of fun when the occasion would allow. He was to settle at Stoke and though critical of some of Matt Gillies' decisions, there did seem a mutual respect between the two. At Stoke it sounds like Tony Waddington had a great deal more going for him than history suggests. While one is often reminded of the Bill Shanklys, the (Sir) Matt Busbys and the Bill Nicholsons, there was a breed of manager not so well known who were also working with their players to produce for the fans – and with Tony Waddington, names like Ron Greenwood and Ted Bates spring to mind. And though the coaching side of club management was moving into a more tactical climate, Gordon is at pains to point out that the more experienced players knew what to do.

There were the usual comings and goings in the close season, but nothing spectacular. Tony Waddington had worked long and hard at Stoke to build them up into a team to be reckoned with. His idea of a team was one balanced with youth and experience, and he was forever looking for great players who had a good season or two left to slot into his side; Gordon being the exception with a good few years left in the tank.

One thing the FA introduced that summer was the 'four steps rule'. This was to combat some goalkeepers (that Gordon argued were not in the English Football League) wasting time by taking possession of the ball and not clearing it. The rule was, however, mainly interpreted that the goalkeeper could take a maximum of four steps while he *held* the ball – most goalkeepers thereafter would dribble the ball in the area and pick it up to make their clearance; this would not answer the question of time wasting. The rule was never formally abolished but today the goalkeeper can only hold the ball for a timed period, but as the referee can add time on for what he considers time wasting, then the rule is as redundant as ever.

Gordon was quoted to have called the rule 'four steps of hell', and thought it would make the problem worse. It certainly did not solve the problem. Other top goalkeepers were as scathing and the referees were not altogether in favour.

The 1967/68 season kicked off and was to be Gordon's first full season with Stoke City. They travelled down to Highbury where Arsenal's Jon Sammels and George Graham took the points. Gordon's performance was described 'a couple of un-World Cup activities by Gordon Banks', which does not say a lot.

Stoke drew with Sheffield United and defeated Manchester City at The Victoria Ground; and then lost away at Sheffield United before they drew at Newcastle. They beat Leicester City 3-2 before they shared points but no goals with West Bromwich Albion. In total they played seven matches in September 1967. Watford came up for a Football League Cup tie but were defeated, and at Chelsea the following Saturday, Stoke managed a draw before beating Southampton at home 3-2. At Anfield, they were defeated by Liverpool before a high-scoring game against West Ham at Upton Park.

On 11 October, Ipswich Town came to The Victoria Ground and threatened Stoke all through the first half. Ray Crawford scored for the visitors, but Harry Burrows equalised. Gerry Bridgwood got the winner for Stoke.

Burnley beat them 2-0 at home, and when Sheffield Wednesday drew with Stoke at Hillsborough it put Wednesday on top of the League – but they did not have an easy time of it. Harry Burrows put Stoke ahead, but Ron Springett had saved his first attempt. Alan Bloor, Calvin Palmer and Alex Elder were 'magnificent'. Jim McCalliog brought a couple of fine saves from Gordon, and John Fantham had managed to get into a good scoring position for Wednesday, but Gordon was off his line and out to stop him at once. But after two possible let-offs for penalties, Stoke finally conceded an equaliser from John Fantham in injury time.

Stoke beat Tottenham at home 2-1, and in the Football League Cup a goalless draw with Sheffield Wednesday at Hillsborough was followed up when they beat them in the replay, though Gordon was absent. He was in the line-up that went to Elland Road in the next round when Stoke crashed out of the tournament 2-0. Meantime in the League, they suffered three defeats – one at home to Fulham and two away at Manchester United and Leeds. In the run up to Christmas, they beat Everton but lost to Arsenal and Manchester City.

Nottingham Forest took three goals for no return, and 37,577 attended the City ground to see them do it. But that attendance figure was part of a bigger picture, as nearly a million spectators went through the turnstiles that Boxing Day. Something else the 37,577 saw that day was Gordon Banks booked for arguing with the referee.

Newcastle United came to The Victoria Ground in January 1968, and were beaten 2-1. Following on from this, Chelsea came and took both points on 20 January. Gordon thought he was impeded when a corner came over for Chelsea and Alan Birchenall scored. But he did not press the point and simply got on with the game.

In the FA Cup, Stoke were to beat Cardiff 4-1 before crashing out to West Ham United at home. This is a good example where fortunes changed quite quickly, skills and abilities were often simple compliments to luck and confidence: 'topsy-turvy' describes their effects.

Back-tracking slightly to Gordon's 'super-efficient' performance at The Dell two weeks earlier, Ron Davies had nine attempts at goal, and the Southampton manager, Ted Bates, said that altogether Southampton made twenty-seven goal attempts. In the last minute, Ron Davies finally scored, but Harry Burrows and Calvin Palmer had already scored for Stoke.

Compare this with the 3-0 home defeat by West Ham United in the FA Cup: 'West Ham carved Stoke into little pieces in the first half.' Sir Alf Ramsey was at the game and saw Gordon 'in fumbling form', though he did sustain an injury in the game. But the final score was Stoke City nil, West Ham United three. When West Ham came up for a League game a week or so later it was a different story – not an overly inspiring game, but George Eastham was credited to have brought it alive. Gordon saved well from John Sissons and Trevor Brooking; Peter Dobing and John Mahoney got the goals for Stoke. Just as they got to 2-0, Gordon 'brilliantly saved a header from Peter Bennett'. Frank Lampard (senior) struck an attempt too hard for Gordon to hold, but the ball went out for a corner.

One statistic from the 1967/68 season no one in Stoke would want to hear was their seven successive defeats in late February, March and early April. They conceded eighteen goals and scored three. Against Tottenham, although they conceded three goals through an 'apology of a defence', Jimmy Greaves did not get his 300th goal for Tottenham.

On 15 April, Coventry City beat them 2-0 at Highfield Road in a bit of an ill-tempered game, and the referee told both captains to calm their players. But 'Banks was in constantly embarrassing situations' and Neil Martin and John Tudor scored for Coventry. The following day, Coventry City came to Stoke and the result was the end of that losing run – but Stoke were now fighting for First Division survival.

Coventry's George Curtis had 'upended' Gordon and treatment was needed – he injured his leg so Gordon let someone else deal with his dead ball kicks after that. After a corner, Ernie Hannigan caught Gordon off balance for 1-0. Neil Martin brought a full-length save from Gordon before Willie Carr made it 2-0. John Mahoney pulled one back. Neil Martin then scored from a penalty, and Tony Bentley again pulled the game back, now 3-2 in Coventry's favour. In the final minute, Peter Dobing scored to force a 3-3, but it had broken their run of defeats.

Even a 4-0 hammering at Burnley wouldn't now break their spirit. They beat Leeds United at home before travelling to Craven Cottage, where Fulham were fighting for First Division survival. Roy Vernon and Peter Dobing sent Fulham into the Second Division, but paradoxically Matt Busby was at the game to see a young Yorkshireman, Allan Clarke, who finally went to Leicester City for a record fee.

Sheffield United joined Fulham in the Second Division, and with Stoke drawing one and winning three of their last four games they survived. But in eighteenth position and only three points clear, they only just made it.

Sunderland were the first visitors to The Victoria Ground when the new season of 1968/69 got underway on 10 August, but they went back to the North East without points. West Ham had more luck four days later, and a trip to Leeds saw a second defeat; so at the start of the season Stoke City had one win and two defeats. Gordon did not play again for over a month until Stoke travelled to Portman Road, where Ipswich beat them 3-1. The ball went into his net three times that day, three times at Nottingham Forest a week later – which was a drawn match – and three times at home to one for Stoke against Burnley. The run of bad luck seemed to ebb at Everton, but they still lost by 2-1.

Chelsea came up to Stoke on 26 November and gave Gordon his second win of the season. Stoke were strong in defence that day and Chelsea were not allowed anywhere near Gordon's goal. All Chelsea could do was pour in long-range shots, which were acknowledged as a 'pointless exercise' by those in the know. Newcomer David Herd scored for Stoke in the first half, and as Chelsea piled on the pressure they were susceptible to the quick counter-attack. Gordon threw the ball out to Jackie Marsh and he passed up to Peter Dobing who was on his own, but had the presence of mind to make it count.

They managed to get another point away at Tottenham, but that was followed by two successive defeats at Coventry and West Bromwich Albion. Manchester United dropped a point when they came down, and Sheffield Wednesday beat Stoke 2-1 at Hillsborough at the end of November.

They beat Newcastle United on the first Saturday in December, and dropped a point at Burnley on the second. They dropped a point at home to Everton and beat visitors Nottingham Forest on Boxing Day.

Gordon's only League appearance in January 1969 was when Tottenham Hotspur came up to Stoke, and it was Pat Jennings that really saved them a point. The game ended with a 1-1 draw and the goals came in the first half. Terry Venables sent in a low shot, and Gordon dived to his left sent the ball away from goal, but David Jenkins was on hand to score. Two minutes later Alan Bloor set George Eastham off and eventually the ball got to Terry Conroy, who scored.

In the FA Cup, York City came to The Victoria Ground and were beaten 2-0. They managed to slip up against Halifax Town on 25 January and conceded a goal, but the replay went emphatically to Stoke. In the replay, Halifax approached the game with enthusiasm, determination and honest endeavour. But Stoke showed their better class, and Gordon stood between Stoke and trouble. By half-time, Peter Dobing had scored for Stoke and it did not take them long to add through Terry Conroy, who got the third goal too.

After a draw in the League, dropping a point at home to West Bromwich Albion, Stoke were ready for their onward move in the FA Cup. On 12 February, they travelled down to Stamford Bridge in London where they were fast and inventive but eventually went down 3-2, though they came close to earning a replay. After seventeen minutes, Bobby Tambling's shot was one Gordon could only parry, and Alan Birchenall was there to poach. In the thirty-second minute, Peter Osgood curled into Gordon's net. Harry Burrows pulled one back for Stoke about ten minutes into the second half, and Gordon saved 'breathtakingly' from John Boyle a few minutes after the restart. Peter Osgood made 3-1 at sixty-eight minutes. Peter Dobing put Stoke back in the game again, and it was Peter Bonetti who really stopped Stoke from equalising. The final score was Chelsea three, Stoke two, and Gordon did not play again until 1 March.

Gordon and Ursula Banks were pleased to welcome their third child, Julia, into the family in the spring of 1969.

Stoke City enjoyed a goalless draw at Leicester, and at Coventry, after persistent rain had made the pitch a mud bath, the score was a goal each. David Herd put Stoke ahead in the twenty-ninth minute and Coventry did not have much to answer with. In the second half, Brian Shepherd sent in a corner, and a collection of players went up for it. The ball was only half cleared as far as Willie Carr, who scored from the edge of the 18-yard box. Coventry looked for a winner but 'Gordon Banks ... dealt with everything sent at him'.

Stoke beat Wolverhampton Wanderers 4-1, and collected a point on a trip to Old Trafford. Five days later across Manchester at Maine Road, they were beaten by City 3-1.

On 5 April, Ipswich Town came to The Victoria Ground. Peter Dobing put Stoke ahead just before half-time and that looked to be that. But just before full-time, a corner was fisted out by Gordon straight on to Mick Mills' head – and from all of 20 yards the ball went in for the equaliser. David Herd made it 2-1 for Stoke just after the restart.

Two days later they travelled to Liverpool to meet them at Anfield. It was labelled as a 'genial' game, though Roger Hunt sustained one of his rare injuries, which did not help the fact they were four points behind Leeds at the top of the First Division. The game itself raised little in the way of action: 'Banks could not complain of overwork'.

The following day they travelled in the opposite direction for a goalless draw at West Ham. This was their third game in four days, and they were weakened through illness and injury. Mike Pejic made his debut, and Denis Smith was solid at the back. Gordon was described as 'formidable' and showed a sense of positioning and handling hailed as 'genius'.

At Loftus Road, Queens Park Rangers were battling with relegation, and both teams battled the high winds. It was this that led Gordon to make an uncharacteristic mistake, and he missed when he jumped to catch a high ball – this left Mick Leach free to tap the ball into an empty net. Mick made it 2-0 before Ron Hunt gave Stoke a bit of hope when he put through his own goal.

Arsenal came up to Stoke for the penultimate game of the season, and went away with both points. Stoke could have done better in this game, and for the second season with Gordon in goal they were not secure from relegation, even this late in the season. Jimmy Robertson scored a lucky goal when it struck Willie Stevenson and travelled into the goal in a different direction to which Gordon had gone. Harry Burrows equalised just before half-time. In the second half, George Armstrong restored Arsenal's lead, and David Court made it 3-1.

That only left the visit of Sheffield Wednesday on 22 April, which finished in a goalless draw.

Things were beginning to take shape at Stoke, and a brief word here about Tony Waddington. Tony was born in Manchester in November 1924, and was on amateur forms with Manchester United before he joined Crewe Alexandra in the late 1940s – he had been in the Navy during the war. He was wing-half for seven seasons, appearing 193 times and scoring eight goals. This was in the old Third Division (North).

He joined Stoke City in 1952 as coach before he became assistant manager, and in 1960 he was appointed manager. His feeling towards tactics was that a solid defence was an essential, but to win a game a dynamic attacking formation was needed. At the least it made the game more entertaining – he built this around the veteran Stanley Matthews, who returned to Stoke City in the early 1960s.

As the decade wore on, he tended to blend youngsters with seasoned veterans who were still quick enough. Back in the First Division, he picked up Gordon for a song, and the record signing of Peter Dobing from Blackburn and players like Alex Elder, David Herd, George Eastham and Maurice Setters, to name a few, gave him a perfect balance – and reintroducing John Ritchie gave him firepower.

Stoke were to see two FA Cup semi-finals and a Football League Cup final under his management – I'll come back to those a bit later.

Comparing and contrasting is never helpful, but one thing Tony did that Matt Gillies did not was to say 'yes' to the visit of a team from Latin America during a tour of Europe. But this was not any old team – it was Santos with Pelé and Edu. The sides lined up against each other on 23 September 1969, with the leader of the attack, Pelé, tingling in anticipation at facing Gordon Banks. Gordon was still improving, and the following year he proved it to about 40 million people. I'm not sure what the attendance was that night, but fairly early on Pelé sprang up from nowhere to dribble around a couple of players until Gordon groped to save. But the inevitable was to happen – Pelé got the ball just inside the 18-yard box, swerved, turned and beat the defenders, but this time when he fired in his shot Gordon had no chance. John Ritchie equalised, and Jimmy Greenhoff put Stoke in front just before half-time. In the second half, Edu scored after three minutes, and Pelé got the winner ten minutes from time.

When Stoke were on tour 'down under', the players would always be ready for a bit of Tony Waddington magic. In a friendly, the host team were 4-0 down at half-time, thanks to John Ritchie. So at half-time, Tony made a temporary transfer of Gordon to their team. But John Ritchie scored another four goals in the second half!

'Football is the working man's ballet' is is only one 'quote' one can attribute to Tony, although I am unsure whether this is an exact or full quotation. He was always keen to point out that football is a sport but it's played as though it's a battle and this is where, if anywhere, the folk on the pitch can stop the hooligan element. He believed in pure football.

He was held in very high esteem by his players and staff, and Gordon makes special mention of him in his autobiography.

Tony left Stoke in March 1977 after twenty-five years. He went back to Crewe Alexandra for two years in the late 1970s, but returned to Stoke City as an associate director. He died aged sixty-nine in January 1994.

Stoke City got off to a promising start in the 1969/70 campaign with no less than seven League games in August. They won three, drew three and only lost one, which was the first fixture of the season away to Wolverhampton Wanderers.

Their Football League Cup campaign was terminated at Turf Moor on 3 September. Burnley's first goal came when the Stoke defence had what seemed to be a lack of concentration, and Dave Thomas scored. Gordon blocked a close-range shot from Frank Casper on the hour. But just a few minutes later he was there again with a fierce shot that Gordon saved, although he could not hold it and Steve Kindon was there to make it 2-0.

Back in the League, their form was still promising. They lost 3-1 at Crystal Palace, but beat Sunderland at home and West Bromwich Albion away. They lost away at Liverpool, but beat Manchester City at The Victoria Ground. So by the end of September, Stoke City were in eighth position of the League with nine points. One worry was that they conceded six goals in seven games in August, but nine goals in only five games in September.

In October they drew three goals each with West Ham, who were missing a few key players, but Clyde Best was outstanding, as was Trevor Brooking. At half-time, West Ham were 3-0 up, but in this fixture history says wait until the final whistle – Stoke scored three times in the second half to level the scores. Stoke had a goalless draw with Arsenal at home, then beat Sheffield Wednesday away. So it looked by then as though their annual struggle in the relegation zone was not going to happen this year.

In late October, a couple of things happened that made the news. Gordon broke his wrist in training – he was doing the extra training he always had and was practising shot-stopping. John Farmer was quite an able deputy, but he was stretchered off at Everton with badly bruised ribs, and their third choice goalkeeper was suspended! Goalkeeping made the headlines for an ugly reason; Peter Bonetti was hit on the head by a rock away in a Football League Cup tie and he actually lost consciousness. He demanded action from the FA, which was widely supported. Mesh netting was a suggestion; Gordon said he had coins, among other things, thrown at him, and Peter Shilton reported a dart landing near him. Fencing the fans in was not considered an option and the fine wire mesh was not pursued.

Gordon returned to active service in mid-November for a 2-0 away win against Sheffield Wednesday, and a 3-3 draw against Ipswich Town. Newcastle United beat them at home, but a win at Newcastle's arch-enemy Sunderland was next on the agenda. Crystal Palace came up to The Victoria Ground and departed without gaining any points.

Over Christmas, Stoke won one and drew one. Against Derby County on Boxing Day, Harry Burrows scored the only goal of the game from the penalty spot and Gordon saved an effort by John O'Hare with some style. On 27 December, they travelled to The Dell in Southampton for a goalless draw. Southampton had gone twenty games without a win, so were determined to try anything anytime they could see the whites of Gordon's goalposts. He was to make a couple of saves that placed him 'apart from all but a few goalkeepers in the world'.

The match was not good, with lots of fouls, but fortunately not dangerous ones. Mike Channon got in a hard shot that gave Gordon little trouble but must have made his hands tingle.

In the FA Cup third round, 'Gordon Banks saved them' – that was what Oxford United's Gerry Summers said after the match. He saved at the near post from Ken Sheen, and later when Ken looked about to pounce again Gordon took a fierce shot from Colin Harrington. But the match ended goalless, so a replay took place at The Victoria Ground four days later. And again it was not going to go entirely Stoke's way because Graham Atkinson shot Oxford into the lead after fifteen minutes; Gordon was helpless. Willie Stevenson equalised and John Ritchie scored after a shot from Jimmy Greenhoff had rebounded. John Ritchie got the third in the second half, and Ken Sheen pulled one back for Oxford.

In the League they lost at home to Liverpool, but had better luck against Manchester City away. Mike Pejic contained Mike Summerbee, and Colin Bell made little impact – Francis Lee was confined to long-range shots. Stoke had the edge in midfield. Terry Conroy scored after seventy-five minutes, though Manchester City did rally a bit and Gordon saved from Colin Bell, Francis Lee and Alan Oakes.

Against Watford in the fourth round of the FA Cup, Gordon was beaten by a 25-yard drive from Colin Franks for the only goal of the game.

In the League, things were petering out a bit – three draws before a defeat at Tottenham; two draws before a defeat at Chelsea; and a defeat at Newcastle United. Burnley's average age at this time was twenty, and when Stoke City went up to Turf Moor the only player to use his considerable experience was Gordon. Burney scored in the fourth minute;

a shot by Eric Probert went in off the woodwork. Stoke did improve a bit in the second half and Willie Stevenson equalised. But a poor back pass made Gordon come quickly off his line to stop Steve Kindon; the ball hit Gordon's legs and shot up in the air and, not for the first time, centre-half Banks cleared with a great header to cheers, and even applause from the referee.

Over Easter, they beat Sheffield Wednesday but lost to Everton – both at home. In the last three matches of the season, they won away convincingly 3-0 at Coventry but lost at home to Chelsea; Ian Hutchinson put Chelsea ahead when he went through on his own. For Chelsea's second, Eric Skeels and Gordon misunderstood what the other was doing and an own goal was the result. Willie Stevenson scored for Stoke in the fifty-second minute. Peter Houseman centred and Gordon managed to push the ball onto the bar, and when it rebounded Tommy Baldwin struck and hit the bar again!

A mere 11,804 folk attended Stoke's last game of the season, which was against West Bromwich Albion at The Victoria Ground. Gordon was a bit unlucky with the first goal; Jeff Astle tried an overhead kick from a good way out which bounced over Gordon's head and into the goal. In reply, John Ritchie, Mike Bernard and Jimmy Greenhoff scored for Stoke City, and finally Colin Suggett found the net for West Bromwich.

But the domestic game was sidelined as ever in the close season, and the 1970 World Cup was to take place in Mexico.

12

The World Cup Finals Mexico 1970

Not quite the tournament one might hope for, but eventful nonetheless. Sir Alf, Harold Shepherdson, Les Cocker (the Leeds United trainer) and the entourage left England amid a blaze of publicity, and in keeping with other superstars of the age, a number one hit song – something Gordon now likes to tell his grandchildren. However, when the company arrived in South America things went from bad to worse – on and off the field. The South American media suggestion that none of the English players or officials were quite the gentlemen they made out was fed to the Latin Americans. This was not a problem in the couple of games tour prior to the finals beginning, and it mainly consisted of locals making a deafening noise when the players were trying to rest. But by the time they got to Mexico, the gutter press had hyped up their 'bad behaviour' to such a degree that taxis permanently honked their horns and general mayhem took place outside their hotel throughout the night.

What also happened showed Gordon that Bobby Moore was not just a gentleman and superb footballer; he also had the integrity one would find in an English ambassador – by the bucketload.

In a hotel they stayed in, in Columbia, a jewellery shop had a lucrative sideline. They would wait until some celebrity came into the shop and then an allegation was made of shoplifting against them; in the past this had happened and it was reported that some money changed hands to drop the charges. But when they accused Bobby, they bit off more than they could chew. Their story changed; the value of the bracelet he was alleged to have stolen fluctuated violently, and which pocket Bobby slipped it into seemed to move from one side of his jacket to the other – the magistrate dismissed the case. Gordon said that for most people this would have been a major trauma, but Bobby simply rejoined the team with the retention of the World Cup uppermost in his mind. But the gutter press now had even more 'evidence' that the English party were 'animals'.

There were other pressures of playing in that corner of the world. England were to play their group matches in Guadalajara, which is a little over 300 miles north-west of Mexico City. It's several thousand feet above sea level (5,400), which made the air thinner so the ball would travel faster and swerve more than at home. The sun was powerful and the heat it generated posed its own problems; high balls got lost in the sun. The games were scheduled so that European audiences could see them, but the timing of this did not help the players as the clock in Mexico is about five or six hours behind ours. To ensure folk in Europe were tucked up in front of the television by about seven o'clock or so, the games had to be played only a couple of hours after midday, when the heat was its most severe. So with the locals hyped up with all the tabloid hostility, it was no surprise when the crowd for their opening match jeered their arrival on the pitch. Gordon describes the affair quite candidly in *Banks of England*, because with Sir Alf thinking about football and not PR the English were misunderstood.

The last person to score a goal for England in a World Cup match was Geoff Hurst, and he lined up with his fellow veterans Bobby Moore, Alan Ball, Bobby Charlton and Martin Peters. Terry Cooper of Leeds United, Keith Newton and Brian Labone of Everton completed the back four. Alan Mullery of Tottenham joined Alan in midfield, with Manchester City's Francis Lee up front with Geoff. It was Gordon's sixtieth cap, and this put him way ahead as the most capped goalkeeper for England.

The opponents for England's first game in the tournament were Romania, and Sir Alf would have been at pains to point out that in their qualifying group, they actually finished ahead of Portugal. So it was that England started their campaign on 2 June 1970. As in many other games, Gordon's first touch was to take a goal kick.

Emerich Dembrowski had the first shot at Gordon's goal, but it never looked likely to create any great problems. The goal kick was passed back for Gordon's preferred throw out of goal, which found Alan Ball.

Romania did mount attacks, but Martin Peters dispossessed Florea Dumitrache on the edge of the 18-yard box, and Brian Labone made the pass back – but Romania looked alive. Both sides had settled well and passes were accurate.

Terry Cooper put over a cross that went half an inch or so astray, and Stere Adamache in the Romanian goal was just above Geoff Hurst. Soon after this, Geoff was sandwiched by Romanian players and came off the worse. Romania went on the attack down the right flank, and Nicolae Lupescu centred for Mircea Lucescu, who just failed to connect. Keith Newton played the ball out for a corner. Keith was active in the England counter-attack and sent over a long, high cross that Martin Peters was after, but he seemed to be obstructed. However, the free-kick went Romania's way – not the first questionable decision from the Belgian referee.

Florea Dumitrache received the ball on the break, but found himself in the corner faced by Bobby Moore and Alan Mullery. Alan seemed to trip him, which prompted a dramatic dive – the free-kick was defended by a two-man England wall and was just on the edge of the 18-yard box. Mircea Lucescu floated the ball over everyone's head, and it went to the far side of the pitch for a throw. Terry Cooper took a free-kick in a similar position at the other end but little resulted. Francis Lee managed to put Bobby Charlton through, he hit the ball with his left foot but a corner was the prize.

Radu Nunweiler and Alan Ball got into a bit of a tussle in the corner, and a corner was awarded. As the ball came over, Gordon took a bit of a risk and travelled a good way off his line, but did manage to get a hand to it. Bobby Charlton had a right-footed shot saved by Stere Adamache, and a little later Francis Lee hit the bar from a Terry Cooper cross.

As half-time approached, Gheorghe Tataru got a good cross but Brian Labone got it away to Keith Newton. Mircea Lucescu won a corner and Gordon took the ball cleanly. Emerich Dembrowski shot, but it lacked power and Gordon took it comfortably.

At half-time the score was 0-0.

Gordon changed his jersey in the break. One of his back four was injured soon after the restart, Keith Newton was flattened as the ball went for a corner. Within a few minutes, it became clear Keith was too badly incapacitated to play on and his Everton teammate Tommy Wright came on as a substitute. But still the 'dreadful tackles' continued, though Romania were coming under pressure.

One of the best attempts at goal, however, came when Radu Nunweiler tried his luck from about 35 yards, and his shot was dipping and heading for Gordon's top right-hand corner. He leapt and at the last second decided to push the ball over for a corner; it was a good shot and a good save.

Alan Ball chipped the ball into the Romanian 18-yard box. Either Martin Peters or Francis Lee were poised and ready to make an attempt, but Francis found Geoff Hurst in a bit of space, and he took it down and past Lajos Sătmăreanu with his right foot to the edge of the 6-yard box where he shot with his left foot. The shot went goalward and reportedly through Stere Adamache's legs and into the goal to put England into the lead.

Romanian tactics took a turn for the worse and Tommy Wright was the next one to be literally flattened. Mihai Mocanu seemed to be the worst offender, but his antics received scant attention from the referee.

Stere Adamache punched a ball clear, which sent Romania on the counter-attack, but Bobby Charlton caught up with them and made a long pass back from just inside his own half to remind viewers at home and spectators in the stadium that Gordon was still taking part in the match. From his throw, Terry Cooper was away before a Romanian player flattened him too.

A good example of how fast the ball tended to travel in that atmosphere was shown when Emerich Dembrowski shot from right midfield to the right of Gordon's goal. He was taken by surprise and dived late to his right but still managed to save it, although he did not hold it.

Nicolae Lupescu took a corner and pumped a high ball over, which Gordon came off his line for, and even surrounded by three Romanian players he still managed to punch it away for a quick counter-attack.

Martin Peters sent a rocket of a free-kick goalwards, but it went just a few inches over the bar. England were content to keep possession, though it did risk another injury from a foul, but the game tended to lose any spark it might have retained after England took the lead. Late on Geoff Hurst was just wide after connecting well with a corner. Bobby Charlton sent a right-footed shot just inches wide in the closing seconds.

Final score: England one, Romania nil.

The following day the second match of the group was played with Brazil beating Czechoslovakia 4-1, and three days later Romania 2-1 against the Czechs. This effectively put an end to Czechoslovakia's campaign, and their one remaining match was with England.

But England had another match first – Brazil. We received the match in the early evening, so in Mexico it was early afternoon – and hot. Players would lose several pounds in weight during a ninety-minute game. England brought in Tommy Wright who'd come on as a substitute against Romania following Keith Newton's injury.

One always finds the unexpected when looking at history, and one sad tale is the eyesight of two of the players on the pitch that day. Gordon's I have discussed, but with the Brazil's No. 9, Tostão, his sight also forced him to retire from the game at just twenty-seven. He had been hit in the face by a ball some while before the Mexico finals and had surgery – in his case he did get a bit more time playing – but two or three years later he was forced to hang up his boots. He left football and took up medicine, but eventually went into broadcasting and returned to the footballing world in 1997. It was reported that after the 1970 final, Tostão gave his medal to the surgeon who had saved his sight – I'm quite sure Gordon knew how grateful he felt. It was not until a couple of weeks before the team left for Mexico that he was given the all clear. He later said that in the final he did not see the final goal as he was weeping with joy for the final few minutes.

But back-tracking to England's tie with Brazil. The match came to be known as Bobby Moore's greatest, and it was the one where Gordon made that save against Pelé – and on the subject of sight, I don't think anyone ever really believed that ball did not go in. But it did not. I will not do too much on something most people in the world have seen, but as it has been called the 'save of the century' there seems little choice!

And again a solid back four of Terry Cooper, Tommy Wright, Brian Labone and Bobby Moore tend to make the biographer's job a little more difficult. But the ball was in motion, the game had started and the World Champions were on the attack. Martin Peters got a shot in, but Félix in the Brazilian goal was there. A Bobby Moore free-kick looked to be destined for Geoff Hurst's head, but Geoff could not connect well enough.

A big boot upfield from Carlos Alberto on the five-minute mark nearly found Pelé, and Gordon was yet to get his first touch. But he did get his first touch from a back pass to stop a Pelé-led attack.

Bobby Charlton nearly managed to break through, but the ball was marshalled back to Félix, whose concentration seemed to have improved. And Francis Lee put in a long-range shot/cross that Félix collected comfortably before rolling the ball along the ground to Carlos Alberto. Carlos accelerated and took the ball towards the halfway line and played the most extraordinary ball forward with the outside of his right boot. When the ball hit the ground it seemed to spin off at an angle – a snooker player can put 'side' on the cue-ball to make it behave in a particular way, and this is what seemed to happen. It went across in front of Terry Cooper, but Jairzinho seemed to anticipate what was going to happen. He accelerated towards the goal line. Poor old Terry had been left standing and Jairzinho centred. Tostão was on the 6-yard line, but it was far too high for him and Pelé was already up – Tommy Wright was still on his way up. When Pelé made contact with the ball it was a perfect header, but more, it was an intelligent header because it hit the ground and bounced towards Gordon's goal. Pelé turned away – job done. His hands went up as he waited for the cheer of the crowd. Gordon, though, had other ideas – he had crossed the goalmouth in less than an instant and dived to his right and rear. He got a hand to the ball and over the bar it went. Whether it was the best save of the century is not really open to question – the best striker/player in the world against the best goalkeeper, something a bit special is bound to happen. At home all we could do was look on in awe.

The Brazilians were not overly confident, and when England attacked their defence was quickly bolstered by their midfield. But passes were going astray from both sides. Francis Lee was fouled but the ref blew late; a quickly taken free-kick soon saw Bobby Charlton through, but Félix was out to meet him. Tommy Wright centred to see Martin Peters head following Francis Lee's flick on.

A couple of times the ball travelled across Gordon's 18-yard box, but the Brazilians did not have anyone there. Alan Mullery sent Tommy Wright to the goal line and he crossed; Francis Lee put in a perfect header for Félix to save but he did not hold it and took quite a knock when Francis followed up.

A couple of corners brought a masterful catch from Gordon as Pelé waited to score. Rivelino and his left foot took a free-kick just outside the angle of the 18-yard box but before Gordon could get near it, Bobby Moore had played the ball out.

Gordon stopped a chance for Tostão by taking out a cross.

Half-time: 0-0.

Tostão kicked off the second half for Brazil, who were soon on the attack. Carlos Alberto took the ball up and centred: 'Banks read that like an open book.' Francis Lee got in a shot but it was straight at Félix. The Brazilian defence did come under a little pressure, and Brito rather roughly pushed Martin Peters off the ball. Brazil were slow to build up an attack, but Paulo César got in a good right-footed shot that Gordon saved with a left dive. Pelé put through a long ball for Jairzinho to chase – as it bounced Gordon was about 10 yards from it and Jairzinho about six, but Gordon just got there first and cleared for a throw-in. Hugh Johns thought he was brave to come that far out of his goal; Gordon indicated to the referee that Jairzinho's boot was too high. It was.

As the second half settled, England started to come under pressure. Pelé got through several tackles before Alan Mullery put the ball out. Rivellino let a shot go with his atomic left foot that Gordon had not only anticipated, but saved superbly. Unfortunately, he could not hold it, but if he'd been a couple of stones lighter the ball would have carried him with it into the back of the net, and probably beyond.

Tostão came alive and dangerous. He made a run towards the area, elbowing Alan Ball in the process. He passed Tommy Wright and Bobby Moore before he turned and centred the ball; to Pelé, who passed to his right where Jairzinho was on the run. He took it to the 6-yard box as Gordon came galloping out of his goal, but Jairzinho's shot got the better of him. But it was Tostão who had done the work, he picked just the right moment to come alive. 'Banks had no chance.'

Bobby Charlton nearly equalised in the next attack. Jeff Astle and Colin Bell came on for Francis Lee and Bobby Charlton. Brain Labone and Bobby Moore were caught short as Jairzinho made for Gordon's goal again, but Bobby Moore took the ball off him with the most skilful, well-timed tackle imaginable.

Straight back up t'other end through Colin Bell and out to Terry Cooper, who put in a long cross thst fell to Everaldo's right foot, but he sliced it without power and it went straight to Jeff Astle's left foot whose effort went wide as Félix advanced.

Jeff was just unlucky – he did not miss it as Hugh Johns suggested, and I gather David Coleman for the BBC was even more scathing; it's about what Jeff did not do, and that was score. So often people have said he had only just came on for Francis Lee but that is only a fact, it isn't an analysis. Others have offered the fact that he did not have time to think – Terry Cooper did cross long and high so the ball fell sharply from over Jeff's head to Everaldo's feet about 4 yards away. Jeff had stopped his forward momentum and was almost waiting for the clearance so he could start thinking about the next attack. The last thing he would have expected was a 'perfect' pass from Everaldo, so when he did get it he gave an instinctive attempt at goal. It went wide. In a million and one cases, he would have scored; that was his million and two. I'd love to know what Sir Alf was thinking. When the dust settled and the game continued, it was described as a 'terrible miss' – that added cruelty to the insult to the injury.

No. 13, Roberto, came on for Tostão. Colin Bell got sandwiched in the 18-yard box, but play went on. England lacked a goal; their belief in themselves was so clear and aptly demonstrated when Alan Mullery headed down for Gordon as Pelé advanced.

Jeff Astle was one of the most powerful headers of the ball, and he headed down for Alan Ball to strike, but it hit the bar. Luck was not with them.

Paulo César got in a powerful shot that Gordon saved comfortably: with only ten minutes left. Substitute Roberto let go with a fierce shot following an excursion upfield from Clodoaldo, but diving down to his right, Gordon made a good save. England poured forward, Brazil defended.

Final score: Brazil one, England nil.

Anyone who liked football, no matter who they thought were the best in the world, could only watch on with awe as these two teams battled it out in the heat. Even the referee, Abraham Klein, said later that he did not trouble too much when he blew his whistle for full-time and the game continued, because no one heard him! So that seems to be a bit of a bonus: 'It was such a great game I let it continue for a few minutes.'

The final group game for England, still on two points, was a game they needed to draw at minimum. Czechoslovakia had not enjoyed a good tournament and were bottom of the group without any points. Brazil had demolished them and Romania had defeated them; Ladislav Petrás had scored both of their goals.

So in the searing heat of Guadalajara, there were a few changes to the side; Keith Newton was fit again at left-back, Jack Charlton came into central defence, Colin Bell in midfield, and Jeff Astle with Allan Clarke up front. Gordon got his first touch when he collected a ball Keith Newton had chested down. For the first ten minutes or so, it was clear there was tension in the English side, concentration was poor and passes were going astray. Jozef Adamec took a corner that swung inwards, and Keith Newton was positioned on the near post to clear off the line. It was interesting to see the goalmouth set up under Gordon's directions – Keith at the near post with Gordon in the centre of the goal and Terry Cooper at the far post. It looked efficient and was effective.

The England defence continued promisingly, but in the first thirty minutes or so the midfield and forward line were not connecting with each other. The first half proved to be a disappointing display, and allowed Czechoslovakia too much opportunity to get around the English defence.

At half-time the score was 0-0.

But they did start to put together a couple of moves in the early part of the second half. Keith Newton joined in an attack and slotted a ball through to Colin Bell inside the 18-yard box; Vladimír Hagara challenged. Both fell but Vladimír controlled it with his left hand, so a penalty. Allan Clarke converted the penalty.

Things improved spasmodically, but the match commentator Hugh Johns said, 'Some of this English passing is too bad to be true.'

Peter Osgood came on for Jeff Astle just about on the hour.

Ladislav Petrás took a free-kick from just outside of the 18-yard box that Gordon tipped over the bar. But the Czechoslovakians looked as unlikely to score as England did in increasing their lead, although Colin Bell netted but was offside. Alan Ball came on as a substitute for Bobby Charlton.

With fresh legs on things picked up a bit, but Ivo Viktor in the Czechoslovakian goal was efficient. Bobby Moore took over from Jack Charlton marking Ladislav Petrás – he was fast, gifted and twelve years younger than Jack! But he managed to get away from Bobby and made an excellent through pass for the Czechoslovakian substitute Karol Jokl, who shot on the run, but Gordon had anticipated his move and dealt with it.

Alan Ball hit the bar – again. Ladislav Kuna came in for a free-kick and headed just wide, but it was clear the defence had got a bit slack.

A rare occurrence – and the only real example of Gordon losing concentration – was when full-back Karol Dobias let fly from about 35 yards. Gordon did not catch or punch it over, he just seemed to stand there and the ball hit his hands, or at any rate that's what seemed to happen. The ball went up and rebounded off the crossbar before Jack Charlton could safely control it for Gordon to then take possession of!

'What a let-off for England.'

Jozef Adamec put a free-kick just wide.

Final score: England one, Czechoslovakia nil.

So from the group, England joined Brazil for the quarter-finals. England were off to León, which is west of Guadalajara and more centrally north-west from Mexico City, to face West Germany in the quarter-finals. Five veterans from the German side of four years earlier were there, and five from England's team.

These days no end of provision would be made for the dietary requirements of the players. But while England took their own food, the Mexican authorities would not allow it into the country, so the squad were catered for by the hotel. This went without a serious hitch, although Alan Mullery said it still turns his stomach when he thinks of the bill of fare. But one problem that did emerge was that Gordon went down with a severe case of what the doctor diagnosed as food poisoning. Was it something he ate or something he drank? Some of the other players had mild symptoms that cleared up quite quickly; they had all eaten largely the same meals, and the drinks were not excessive but a treat. So was it something Gordon ate or drank? Whatever it was, the symptoms persisted and were severe – as well as 'one end', one can also suffer the 'other end'. This can also be accompanied by digestive pains, and without the ability to retain food and fluid one can feel very ill and weak – and become very ill and weak, as dehydration would be a major concern. Not the best of situations for a sportsman, especially in an unfamiliar climate. Gordon was ruled as unfit to play and Peter Bonetti of Chelsea was to deputise.

England took the lead just after the half-hour through Alan Mullery following a Keith Newton cross. Martin Peters added to the lead four minutes into the second half – again with Keith feeding superbly. By now the weakness had taken its toll on Gordon, and he fell asleep with England two up. England looked comfortable, but Franz Beckenbauer pulled a goal back on sixty-eight minutes. On seventy minutes, Bobby Charlton was substituted and Colin Bell came on; some said this was the turning point in the match, but Colin was one of the world's greatest players and at that time would have been the equal to Bobby. What was going through Sir Alf's mind at the time, this is the core of the question because a substitution is to strengthen a team and Sir Alf knew what he was about. And the German fight-back had already started – something Bobby Charlton will usually point out. It was just one of those unfortunate things that Uwe Seeler got the equaliser six minutes later. At ninety minutes, the game was all square as Gordon slept in the hotel. One of the best players ever to grace the German game, Gerd Mueller, got the winner just after the start of the second period of extra time. England were no longer World Champions, inevitably Gordon woke and heard the news.

Bobby Charlton had won his 106th cap, which set a record, but it was his last game for England. It was also the last World Cup finals game for Sir Alf, as England did not qualify in 1974. Sir Alf cursed the luck that had run out for England and was quoted to have said that of 'all players to lose … it had to be him'. Gordon later said it would be 'impossible to say' that if he had played it would have made a difference.

As to whether Gordon's food or drink were tampered with is a difficult question. His first reaction was that this was unlikely, but with the passing of time his resolve against it has shifted. So many people have commented on it that any clear thought from Gordon simply has ceased to be possible because of the sheer amount of oars to steer his boat. It is possible he did something different, but after all this time, who knows what?

Simply, England were beaten. There are theories as to why, but I think the luck just was not with them that day. If form was anything to go by, England should have beaten them – Italy did and then were demolished by Brazil in the final – Brazil had only just beaten England, or more accurately, England had only failed to score.

Brazil won the tournament and as it was their third victory – the Jules Rimet Trophy became theirs outright. However, back at Rio it was stolen and was never recovered. One report said, 'no sooner had Carlos Alberto returned it to Rio', which would put the theft as 1970, but other reports suggest it was 1983 when it went. If it was 1970 then Pickles was still basking in glory, but by 1983 he may have been cocking his leg at the pearly gates.

13

After Glory Came More Glory

So with the disappointment of the World Cup behind him, and the 'did I get, or was I given food poisoning' firmly on his 'One Hundred Questions to Answer Before I'm Ninety-Nine' list, the more modest heat of an English autumn saw Gordon don his No. 1 shirt for Stoke City to start the 1970/71 season.

The next two seasons were successful for Stoke insofar as they had good cup runs. And there was a trophy in the not-too-distant future, and a Wembley-won cup victory at that. In the League and FA Cup, this was to be Arsenal's year to emulate their rivals' (Tottenham Hotspur) achievement of the double – the League championship and FA Cup wins in the same season.

Stoke City's Wembley win was to be in the Football League Cup in the 1971/72 season, but their run in the competition in the 1970/71 season was not spectacular.

In the League they were to finish way above the relegation danger zone so it looked like, and Gordon echoes this in his autobiography; Tony Waddington's long struggle to make Stoke City a foremost club was well on its way. As a player, Gordon was at his peak and he should have had a good many seasons left. In total he played fifty League and cup games in the 1970/71 season.

His first appearance was at The Victoria Ground for a visit from Ipswich Town – a luke-warm affair with little excitement until the last minute. Clive Woods, travelling at speed, shot from the edge of the 18-yard box for Gordon to dive; twisting backwards across the goal to steer the ball safely out of play. Clive said Gordon had taken off very late and the ball seemed to have passed him! Nevertheless, 0-0.

Four days later, Stoke added two points with a convincing 3-0 home win over Newcastle United. Derby County beat them 2-0 at the Baseball Ground – where Gordon may have picked up a slight injury to his thigh.

Stoke then made the short journey to West Bromwich Albion, and were beaten 5-2 – the first time Gordon had been beaten five times in a match since March 1967. He put in extra training and said, 'It mustn't happen again.' It did not.

Two clean sheets followed in goalless draws against Crystal Palace and Nottingham Forest at home, and a 1-1 draw away to Wolverhampton Wanderers. Then in the Football League Cup, Second Division Millwall came up to Stoke and had a ball. Doug Allder and Steve Brown tested Gordon from all angles, and a couple of long-range shots came in from Steve Brown again and Eamon Dunphy. The game was marred by a sending-off and a booking. Gordon had sustained a groin strain, so he missed the replay in London, which Millwall won; he was also sidelined for Stoke's 5-0 hammering of Arsenal.

There was some suggestion Gordon was still a bit short of total fitness after the tummy bug that summer in Mexico, but he clarified it had been the groin strain. Before the Millwall defeat, they had beaten the then mighty Leeds United 3-0 at home; in their next away match Manchester City beat them 4-1.

After their exit from the Football League Cup and Gordon's lay-off, he was back for 1-1 draw at Blackpool, and a 2-1 home win over West Ham United. It was then reported that Brazil wanted to secure Gordon's services as a goalkeeping coach for their youngsters, but Albert Henshall, the Stoke chairman, suggested this might be for the close season. Nothing came of it.

In mid-October, Stoke travelled to Portman Road in Ipswich to be beaten 2-0, and for the first time since Boxing Day 1967, Gordon was booked. As for a match report, the newspapers would report that Gordon had 'performed his customary wonders'. It was a dreadful afternoon – Peter Dobing broke his leg and Tony Waddington reported the match referee to the FA. Comments were heard at Liverpool Street station in London on the return journey. It all blew over.

The following week, Stoke travelled to Tottenham where Willie Stevenson broke his leg! Gordon became captain in the absence of Peter Dobing. Martin Chivers scored twice for Tottenham; one goal being a Brazilian-type banana shot which, although it beat him, Gordon was quick to praise. Alan Gilzean scored the other goal for Tottenham. Martin Peters was at the top of his form and Gordon was stretched to make two good saves from him. Cyril Knowles, Jimmy Pearce and Steve Perryman also brought out 'breathtaking' saves from Gordon.

As winter approached, Stoke beat Huddersfield Town 3-1, drew away 2-2 at Manchester United, and shared the points with a goal apiece at home to Everton.

Leeds United four, Stoke City one was the scoreline on 18 November, and it was Stoke City through Terry Conroy who scored first. Paul Madeley equalised but there was some question of a foul on Gordon. Allan Clarke put Leeds ahead. A controversial penalty five minutes from time by Johnny Giles – twice taken because the referee thought Gordon had moved – was complimented by Peter Lorimer just before time. It was said that Stoke's defence was quite magnificent, and one can't help thinking of the foul on Gordon; if there was one and the penalty incident, then what the score might have been. But nothing can ever be taken away from the Leeds attack in those days – superb doesn't even do them justice.

Stoke's remaining two fixtures in November were a 2-1 defeat at Chelsea, and a goalless draw at home to Southampton.

In December, Stoke travelled to Coventry, who came out on top 1-0.

Rewinding six months or so; everyone will marvel at the Pelé save with Gordon's speed and agility and everything else to be seen. What is not seen is the anticipation of what the player is going to do and then what the ball is going to do. In mid-flight Gordon saw Pelé's header and could anticipate where it would hit the ground and then bounce up – so at the last millisecond, after the ball has bounced, he can consider its final path and act, which he did by pushing it over the bar. In talking about the save, Gordon will often discuss the ground on which the game was played; he will often make a good inspection of the ground before the match, and in particular what effects the ground might have on a ball.

But at Coventry that day he was not thorough. John O'Rourke headed the ball and Gordon had to, as ever, anticipate what the ball was going to do – but it did not do as he had anticipated and did not bounce as he thought it would. Instead it trickled through his fingers and into the net. He made some great saves after this, from John O'Rourke again, then Dave Clements and Dennis Mortimer. But with the terrain error and an out-of-luck strike force, it meant victory for Coventry.

The week before Christmas and Derby County came to Stoke, where the visitors were defeated by a goal to nil. Gordon's clean sheet was threatened by Kevin Hector, but he made a good save. On Boxing Day, they stole a point from Liverpool at Anfield, but it was not easy – Gordon saved a strong header from John Toshack and pushed a Phil Boersma cracker round the post. Liverpool had a goal disallowed, and both Denis Smith and Jackie Marsh cleared off the line.

Stoke's good FA Cup run of that season said as much about their character, spirit and stamina as it did about their skill. And they were again at the hands of Second Division Millwall, who scored after three minutes! John Ritchie equalised and Jimmy Greenhoff put them into the fourth round.

The first Saturday of January is often where the higher clubs join the cup run, but up in Scotland one tradition for their New Year – Hogmanay (strictly speaking the end of the *old* year) – is an 'old firm' clash between Glasgow Rangers and Celtic, which that year finished with a 1-1 draw. The match had been scoreless until the closing stages, and some fans were making their way out of the ground; up went the roar and some supporters turned to head back into the ground. The rush became a crush, a fatal crush. Gordon with Bobby Charlton (England) and George Best (Northern Ireland) along with Wyn Davies (Wales) joined a Celtic and Rangers select XI to play the Scottish national side in the form of a testimonial. The score is immaterial, but in the Ibrox disaster sixty-six souls perished.

Normally in the FA Cup, the First Division sides would find their way through to the later rounds, but this is not always the case. If luck goes with the winning club, then when they start their campaign in the third round they are six matches away from victory; 540 minutes of play. For Stoke that year they did not make the final, but they played an incredible 840 minutes of football! This involved three replays and a second replay – one with extra time. At home to Huddersfield Town in the fourth round, the game finished 3-3, but the replay at Leeds Road finished goalless even after extra time. Stoke won the second replay 1-0. At home to Ipswich in the fifth round, the result was a goalless draw, but Stoke won the replay at Portman Road – the game was described as 'crude and crunching' with a total of forty-three fouls. But it was reported that Gordon was on top form, making numerous top-class saves – some which were described as magnificent. On right dives he denied Colin Viljoen and Peter Morris; diving left he stopped Mick Mills, John Robertson and Peter Morris again – Gordon went backwards to stop Mick Hill from scoring. Ipswich manager, Bobby Robson, described him as 'superb'.

In the sixth round, Hull City were two goals up before Stoke got into their stride and came back to win 3-2.

Things had moved on in the League with an away win at Newcastle and a home win against West Bromwich Albion in January, where they finished the month beaten 2-1 at Southampton. On duty for England in early February, Gordon was injured but was back for the Huddersfield Town second replay and the Ipswich Town ties.

Future Stoke star Alan Hudson came up to The Victoria Ground with Chelsea and saw a brilliant individual goal disallowed – but Tony Waddington said they were superb throughout. Terry Conroy put Stoke ahead for Chelsea to equalise – Chelsea's winner came after a goalmouth mix-up. A draw at Burnley and a single-goal win away to Huddersfield prepared them for their win at Hull, as described, in the sixth round of the FA Cup – next it was Arsenal who they had beaten 5-0 earlier in the season.

In mid-March, in the League, Everton beat them 2-0 at Goodison Park, and Gordon injured his right knee. But he was back in time for Manchester United's successful visit to Stoke, winning 2-1.

Then it was Arsenal in the FA Cup semi-final at Hillsborough. By now his old teammate from his Leicester City days, Frank McLintock, captained Arsenal; they had both played in two FA Cup finals and been on the losing side, so it was hoped that one of them would be lucky third time round. Tony Waddington said his side would be 'Gordon Banks and ten others!'

The game finished all square at two goals each, but Stoke had been two up at half-time. Gordon had made a great save from Ray Kennedy and would deny George Graham in the second half. Peter Storey pulled a goal back for Arsenal, and in the last few seconds they were awarded a penalty. Up stepped Peter again: 'I usually put them to the 'keeper's right. Then I thought … this is Banksie. He'll know that. So in the other side it goes.' And it did.

Four days later at Villa Park, Arsenal came out winners at 2-0. They were better on the night; Gordon aggravated a hamstring injury and missed the next game against Crystal Palace. But the cup run had given them a backlog of League fixtures, and the Palace game was one of seven that April! Excluding the Palace fixture, they won two, drew one and lost one at home, and lost one and drew one away.

By early May, Arsenal were gunning for the title and FA Cup double when they welcomed Stoke City to Highbury. Arsenal could not afford to even drop a point, let alone get beat, and they scraped through 1-0.

Martin Peters scored with a 30-yard lob that went over Gordon's head and in off the post in their final game of the season at home to Tottenham. He had timed his run to perfection and was a half-inch or so onside when the ball was played.

Stoke beat Everton 3-2 – despite being two down early on in the FA Cup third place play-off. Alan Ball hit the post with a penalty, the first that season for Everton!

One sad incident in the close season saw Gordon, Bobby Charlton and Bobby Moore on club tours, so were unable to join a Rest of World XI for Lev Yashin's testimonial. Pelé too was unable to play due to club commitments. Not one of those players would have missed it if they could possibly have helped.

All too soon Stoke City were travelling to Highfield Road, Coventry, for a 1-1 draw to start the 1971/72 season. Coventry should have won this; Willie Carr missed an open goal. John Ritchie hit the equaliser to Ernie Hunt's earlier score. Thereafter Stoke made an unsuccessful attempt to gain points from Southampton at The Dell.

Finally, or so it must have seemed, Peter Dobing made his return for a 3-1 victory at home to Crystal Palace. Gordon's old club, Leicester

City, who had just returned to the First Division, were defeated in a quite 'mediocre game', but did score first; John Ritchie soon equalised and Mike Bernard and Peter Dobing finished the job off. But Gordon took quite an active part saving long-range efforts from Rodney Fern and Len Glover.

As September approached, Stoke went to Highbury where they took both points from a disappointing Arsenal. They also took a point from Nottingham Forest at the City Ground, but lost 1-0 to Wolverhampton Wanderers at The Victoria Ground. Derby County hammered them 4-0, but they took both points off a visiting Huddersfield Town.

Their last fixture in September was to be the first of a number of encounters with West Ham United. Clyde Best dazzled the crowd and won the admiration of Tony Waddington, but Gordon had to retrieve the ball twice from his net; once from Clyde but also Bobby Moore of all people, though Gordon deserved better luck when Bobby's shot cannoned off Denis Smith and went over his head.

Stoke City at home to Liverpool in early October saw no goals, but clearly Sir Stanley Matthews' claim that a strong Stoke was to emerge in the early 1970s was beginning to show itself.

They travelled to Oxford for their first of nineteen cup ties. Jimmy Greenhoff opened Stoke City's Football League Cup account. John Evans was prominent for Oxford that night, getting the equaliser and also bringing a fine save from Gordon.

Two League wins followed, against Sheffield United at Bramall Lane and at home to Coventry. Gordon had a fitness test on his knee, but he was fit for Stoke's defeat of Oxford in the replayed cup-tie at The Victoria Ground. The word 'majestic' described one of his saves from Oxford's Dave Sloan. John Ritchie and Sean Haslegrave sent Stoke to Old Trafford for the next round.

When I discussed the total games Gordon or Stoke City played that year it did not include minor tournaments, and one they participated in was the Texaco Cup. Gordon put up a good display in a tie with Derby County, though it was Derby who went on to the next round.

Three days before their meeting with Manchester United in the Football League Cup, Stoke travelled to Ipswich where a tummy bug was said to have weakened the hosts. Nevertheless, Ipswich put on a fine display winning by two Mick Hill goals to a Mike Bernard goal for Stoke.

Away to Manchester United, Alex Stepney put on a magnificent display. But that did not stop Stoke getting a 1-1 draw courtesy of John Ritchie with Alan Gowling replying for United with a glancing header with only five minutes left. Gordon had done well to deny George Best and Denis Law. It sounded as though Gordon was as ever quick to start counter-attacks as United surged forward.

A League win at home to Tottenham and an away win at The Hawthorns filled the gap before the Football League Cup replay with Manchester United. This was a goalless affair even after extra time, Gordon made a great save from Sammy McIlroy, and he punched out a header from Willie Morgan that was right on target. John Ritchie had a goal disallowed and an Alan Bloor effort was cleared off the line.

Chelsea came up for a League match that saw a quite remarkable goal from Peter Osgood; Gordon was a mere onlooker and said, 'It was a really fine shot and I hadn't a chance to clear it.' Tony Waddington had a job to contain his fury as Stoke were denied a penalty and had a goal disallowed. It was said that Peter Bonetti was almost nailed to his posts as Stoke strived for an equaliser – luck just was not on their side. They scored a goal which everyone, except the referee, thought was a perfectly good goal.

In mid-November, they met Manchester United for the Football League Cup replay. Alan Gowling passed through to George Best, who was just onside, and from 12 yards he does not miss and goalkeepers did not often stop him. Peter Dobing went on to equalise, and John Ritchie got the winner about two minutes from time.

Leeds United took both points at Elland Road before Stoke travelled south for a tie with Bristol Rovers to further their quest for the Football League Cup. In the rain-sodden shadow of the M32, the crowd saw a textbook performance to defeat a Third Division Bristol Rovers. Rovers scored two late goals that were described as a 'spurious act of defiance'. Harold Jarman though did bring out a 'world-class save' from Gordon, and he also managed to tip a looping shot from Wayne Jones over the bar. Later he bravely dived at Robin Stubbs' feet to rob him of a shooting chance.

A 3-3 draw with Newcastle United at home, and a goalless draw at Everton followed. As the Football League Cup semi-finals approached, Gordon went on record as saying that Stoke City would go flat-out to reach Wembley after the previous season's disappointment in the defeat by Arsenal in the FA Cup semi-finals.

With skill, courage and luck, West Ham took the first leg 2-1 – Peter Dobing scored first for Stoke. Geoff Hurst equalised from the penalty spot – Gordon learns from everyone – and Clyde Best scored the winner from Harry Redknapp's cross.

Manchester United came down to Stoke for a 1-1 draw, and the preparations for the second leg of the League Cup semi-final was on their minds; a goal down with the away leg to consider.

Stoke won 1-0; John Ritchie scored the only goal of the game. As I said above, Gordon learns from everyone; in the first leg West Ham were again awarded a penalty and in extra time in the second leg they were awarded a penalty – just a few minutes from the end. So it was Geoff Hurst *v.* Gordon Banks. But Geoff made the same preparation as he did for the penalty at The Victoria Ground – the same long run up. Was it going to Gordon's right again? There was nothing for it but to dive right, and as he lifted up his right hand the ball struck and went over the bar! Gordon said a couple of years later that he imagined Geoff with fire coming from his nose and quipped that he really intended to get out of the way! But save it he did, and Stoke City and West Ham United would have to slog it out again.

Stoke lost 2-0 at Wolverhampton Wanderers the week before Christmas, and on Boxing Day Manchester City won at The Victoria Ground 3-1. On New Year's Day, they took a point at Huddersfield.

On 5 January, Stoke made the trek up to Hillsborough where, after extra time, the scoreline was West Ham United nil, Stoke City nil! Clyde Best could have settled it but Gordon didn't let him; he pounced on the ball in Clyde's possession and the ball went out for a corner. A dreadful back pass from Peter Dobing but West Ham could not capitalise.

There were no goals in Arsenal's League visit to The Victoria Ground, but Stoke did manage to progress in the FA Cup, beating Gordon's old club, Chesterfield, 2-1. Southampton paid a visit and departed after a 3-1 defeat. So, off to Old Trafford for yet another crack at West Ham United in the Football League Cup.

And there was finally a victor: Stoke.

In the bitter cold, the teams gave a magnificent performance epitomising good football. One sad moment was when Bobby Moore lost his footing and let Terry Conroy in, but he collided with Bobby Ferguson in the West Ham goal. Bobby was knocked clean out so Bobby Moore took his jersey while he was getting treatment. And disaster struck; John Ritchie was felled, so a penalty. Mike Bernard *v.* Bobby Moore – and he saved it! But Mike was able to then stroke the ball in the net for 1-0. Billy Bonds put in a 25-yard shot to equalise, so perhaps justice was done. Trevor Brooking gave West Ham the lead on the stroke of half-time.

George Eastham was not settling for that – he set up the equaliser for Peter Dobing. Frank Lampard (senior!) sadly made a slip, and Terry Conroy was not going to give him any chance to recover. Stoke City three, West Ham United two. The four-match-two-extra-time marathon was over.

Three days later, Gordon was back at Filbert Street for his old club (Leicester) to beat his new club. Tranmere Rovers held them to 2-2 in the fourth round of the FA Cup but Stoke won the replay.

Ipswich Town took a point on a visit, and when Stoke paid a visit to Tottenham Hotspur they took nothing away except themselves. They were drawn against Hull City for the second successive season in the FA Cup, but this time at home they were convincing winners at 4-1.

3 March 1972 saw Gordon's penultimate game at Wembley, but this time with his club. History had shown his club visits to this stadium hadn't been too happy; with Leicester City back in the 1960s he had been on the losing side twice. It might be a good omen though, because this time it was the Football League Cup final. The Brian Moore commentary suggested most people would like to see George Eastham collect a winner's medal/trophy – George had contributed a lot to football in his years.

Alan Hudson got the game underway and John Hollins blasted the ball from the centre circle for a goal kick. Both sides needed to settle – Gordon's first touch came from that goal kick. Peter Bonetti's first touch came when Terry Conroy shot from a distance; his second touch was fisting out a Peter Dobing throw in. Peter's third touch came when he pulled the ball out of his own net after Terry Conroy had given Stoke City the lead.

Alan Bloor took out Chris Garland just outside of the 18-yard box; when the kick was taken John Hollins was just wide with his shot. Chris was floored again, which resulted in another free-kick. This time when the ball was centred, Gordon was able to take it.

A corner to Chelsea, and one could see the ball approach Peter Osgood's head, but Gordon took it off him. The ball fell to Ron Harris, who managed to get in a cross that saw Gordon wrong-footed, but the danger passed. From another corner the ball rolled out to Charlie Cooke whose shot was on target, but Gordon was behind it.

Gordon punched a Charlie Cooke cross away with Chris Garland in attendance. A few moments later, Chris Garland took a shot on the turn; Gordon was quickly down to his right. Next it was Peter Osgood heading towards goal, but Gordon was down again, this time to his left. Chelsea were going all out for the equaliser.

Gordon's luck failed him when Charlie Cooke chipped in, Peter Osgood tried to shoot but fell, and David Webb could not get a shot in as three Stoke City players – Mike Bernard, Denis Smith and Alan Bloor – tried to get the ball away. But they did not and Peter Osgood was able to kick the ball along the ground and into the net.

So at half-time the score was one goal each.

John Ritchie had the ball in the net just after the restart, but was ruled offside. Stoke City started the second half far more determined and were not going to let the goal on the stroke of half-time upset their momentum. The game was evenly balanced with both sides coming forward, and even though there had been a couple of clumsy fouls in the first half and bookings, the second half was an attractive display.

There was only one goal in the second half; every Stoke supporter was delighted and every Chelsea fan must have thought that if they were to go down, then it should be from a goal by the veteran campaigner. And after all he had done for football generally – the neutrals must have thought it was a poetic conclusion for George Eastham to get the winner. Peter Bonetti only parried Jimmy Greenhoff's shot, and George was there to poach.

With twenty minutes left, Chelsea came storming back. John Hollins took a long throw. Gordon fisted it but the ball was played straight back in with John Dempsey on the 6-yard line – Gordon was quickly out. The ball flew across the goal towards Charlie Cooke, but goal kick.

Chelsea piled on the pressure, with big John Dempsey going up for a corner, and he nearly connected. But it looked as though Gordon's face connected with a flailing arm.

Again lady luck seemed to be scheming, and it did not look as though it was going to be Chelsea's day. Another corner, over to the far post where Peter Osgood sent it back across the goal. Gordon made a catch that looked like one of his diving saves to deny the head of both Chris Garland and David Webb.

At the other end, a Terry Conroy corner was met by John Ritchie and Peter Houseman headed off the line.

And then Mike Bernard made the back pass from hell for Gordon to deal with – Chris Garland accelerated like a missile to intercept. Gordon just got there first, but there was a collision.

The final whistle showed the delight of Tony Waddington and Gordon Banks.

Stoke City were not finished in cup competitions yet. On 18 March, they drew one goal each with Manchester United at Old Trafford in the sixth round, and so the tie went to The Victoria Ground four days later. Stoke triumphed 2-1 after extra time and were dubbed 'The Greatest Cup Fighters of The Modern Age'.

Bobby Charlton crossed for Denis Law to head on for George Best, and as he faced Gordon the 'masters stood face to face'. George scored but that did not faze Gordon. Denis Smith went up for George Eastham's corner to equalise. And in the thirteenth minute of extra time, Terry Conroy hammered home from 12 yards. For the second consecutive season they were FA Cup semi-finalists; for the second consecutive season they faced Arsenal.

Derby County paid a visit for a League match and left with a point, and Stoke took nothing away from Liverpool. They took two points at Maine Road against Manchester City, and then there was to be a no-score draw with West Ham at The Victoria Ground. Bill Shankly, the Liverpool manager, was at the match and he said of Gordon, 'the man is absolutely incredible'. Leeds United came to the Victoria Ground and won 3-0.

At Villa Park, Arsenal and Stoke City lined up for the second successive season to fight out the semi-final of the FA Cup and see if Wembley was to beckon. Arsenal for the second time in two seasons, and for Stoke the second time in the current season. Gordon was in tip-top shape, and the only time he was bothered in the first half was by a neat George Graham header that went straight to him. Bob Wilson made a couple of notable saves, but at half-time there was no score.

Come the second half, things plodded a bit but the football was attractive. And when on the edge of the 18-yard box, George Armstrong could just flip the ball up and shoot on the half volley on the semi-turn; Gordon was beaten by a superb goal. Bob Wilson went up for a fairly innocuous cross but seemed to land very badly. He needed treatment, but with a chunk of heavy strapping on his knee he seemed to be okay. That did not last long, and after a brave lunge at the ball when Denis Smith looked to have scored – although Peter Storey was officially attributed to have put it into his own net – the equaliser for Stoke, it was clear Bob's minutes were numbered. John Radford took over in goal and Ray Kennedy came on as substitute. Arsenal had no choice than to form a one-goalkeeper-ten-defenders formation, which helped them survive. The final score was one goal each. Arsenal won the replay 2-1 at Old Trafford, though there was some dispute about an offside for their winning goal.

Three games remained from which Stoke took three points: 1-1 against Everton and West Bromwich Albion at The Victoria Ground, and a goalless draw at St James' Park in Newcastle.

Gordon was elected Sports Writers' Footballer of the Year – he had played fifty-six League and cup games for Stoke City that season out of a total of sixty-seven, not counting friendlies and internationals. Stoke had also participated in the Texaco Cup. As he quipped in his autobiography, 'When you collapsed from exhaustion, you got a game off.'

The 1972/73 season kicked off on 26 August and Stoke had signed West Ham's Geoff Hurst in the summer, which was the usual shrewd move by Tony Waddington of mixing youth with experience.

Everton came down and took a point in a 1-1 draw. Stoke travelled to newly promoted Norwich City and 'only some fine saves by Gordon Banks prevented an even bigger score'. At Coventry three days later, Gordon saved 'their blushes' in a 2-1 defeat.

Stoke City were Football League Cup holders and they started their defence with a comfortable win of 3-0 at home to Sunderland, before the League visit of Leeds United, which ended up at two goals each.

They qualified for the UEFA cup because of their cup success, and their home tie against the German side Kaiserslautern saw them win 3-1.

In mid-September, their fixture against Ipswich Town at Portman Road saw Stoke go down 2-0 in a game marred by poor refereeing decisions. Gordon was out of action until early October when again the opposition was Ipswich at Portman Road – but this time it was in the Football

League Cup and Stoke were winners thanks to goals from John Ritchie and Geoff Hurst; Gordon was said to have 'flung himself everywhere to fight off Ipswich'.

A seven-goal affair at White Hart Lane saw Tottenham as eventual winners, and a week later with the visit of Newcastle United to The Victoria Ground, Gordon's first League clean sheet of the season was achieved.

The headline said it all after Stoke City's away match at Liverpool on 21 October – with Gordon in hospital and second-choice goalkeeper John Farmer in plaster: 'Find a keeper – quick.' Gordon Banks had played the last of his 703 competitive games.

14

Unlucky for Some...

In sport at the level Gordon played, there has to be talent and skill – but there is also no question of total dedication, even if you think as the former Tottenham manager Bill Nicholson did: 'It is better to fail aiming high than to succeed aiming low.'

Put more simply, there was only one place for him to return after his recovery, and that was as goalkeeper for Stoke City. Whether this was going to be possible or not was down to his total dedication; talent and skill plus one other thing, something he could not control, something that had smiled at him on the pitch as often as it had frowned on him – a heavy slice of luck.

Gordon's determination was a sign of his dedication, and throughout his career he would put in the extra training he thought necessary for a goalkeeper. For years he had roped his teammates into helping him with shot training, and the aftermath of the accident and his vision would see him push this up by a good degree. It would take time for one eye to do the job of two, and over the next few years he would tell countless people who had lost sight in an eye that it was perfectly possible to return to life, as they had only temporarily been laid up out of it.

And in Gordon's case there didn't seem to be any reason to doubt this. But if your life happened to be as the best goalkeeper in the world, there had to be questions answered.

But the main thing for the rest of the family was that husband, dad, brother and son was not critically injured, and it was quickly apparent that his injuries were something he could recover from. So the initial return to life for Gordon was fairly straightforward. There was a bit of damage done to his good looks, but that would heal, and the after-accident shock would fade after a few days. The thought that he might have killed or badly injured someone would have been in his thoughts for a good while, and this would have been compounded by the fact that witnesses in their statements had suggested Gordon's driving had not been good. The police later prosecuted him for dangerous driving and he was fined.

However, those were all issues anyone can understand and identify with and work through. What Gordon had to face was the thought that if he was going to continue at the top then a return to complete sight was going to be a prerequisite.

In hospital all went well and his attitude was positive, even though the surgeon only gave him a fifty-fifty chance of his full sight returning. Hope and optimism for any sportsman is a good part of the battle.

But the press didn't help particularly. When the swelling round his good eye subsided and he could see more clearly, then the idea of a television in his room was a boon. In those days NHS hospitals were just not geared up for such luxuries, but the arrangements were made and the television duly arrived.

Meanwhile, Tony Waddington, the Stoke City manager, had called at the house to offer the family what support he could. But he could not get into the place because of the number of press men camped at the bottom of their drive. By now, Ursula was under some pressure and so Tony pleaded with the press to give the family some leeway, and he promised to keep them all informed of progress – which eventually they accepted, and dispersed. But with her husband in hospital and a home with three kids to see to, the pressure on Ursula had increased dramatically.

In hospital, at least, Gordon had some distraction and could watch the television. But the 'engineer' who brought it to him was not an engineer but a journalist, who had spun some yarn to the proper engineer that he was a close friend of Gordon's and could he take the television in. There may or may not have been some money changing hands, but it soon became apparent that his motives were far from proper and Gordon let him know just how much he disapproved of the intrusion.

For most of us, time in hospital with three kids at home can be a real problem, even if time is available to prepare – but an emergency increases the pressure. And having thirty or so reporters besieging your home must make things intolerable.

Journalism is big business and the so-called 'cheque book' journalism was growing in momentum. But the temptation to attract a big money cheque was not a major issue for the Banks family – Ursula wanted Gordon home and Gordon wanted to play football. The kids, no doubt, wanted things to return to normal. Messages of goodwill poured in by the sackful.

Eventually he could be discharged from hospital, but he was to see the surgeon in the outpatients where things continued hopeful, and when the stitches had been taken out there was still a good chance of further improvement. It was the waiting that was the problem. But the operation had been very delicate with damage to the retina, and to enhance recovery 100 micro stitches had been inserted.

However, it did become apparent during this time that even though Gordon returned to full training and could judge crosses and shots, there was still a major problem, as a goalkeeper's lot is to anticipate and judge a situation. The speed of the ball is all-important, as is where a striker may shoot or pass it. Anyone who has seen the save he made against Pelé in Mexico would understand that when Jairzinho crossed the ball, there was the strong possibility that Tostão, who was approaching from a slight left trajectory to Gordon's goal, would be the choice to receive Jairzinho's cross. But the cross was high and deep, so Gordon would soon know Tostão was not the target. Advancing hard from Gordon's right trajectory was Pelé, and he rose to head the ball hard. So Gordon needed all of his vision and judgement of the speed of the ball Jairzinho crossed, where it was likely to go, who was there and what they might do with it – then what they *did* do was what he had to deal with.

Now to bring life from the Mexican sunshine back to the Staffordshire autumn. Gordon tried to pick up a cup filled with good, old hospital tea, but missed it. That tea cup made him pull out all the stops to attempt to make his recovery complete and return to Stoke City's goal. But a few months later when Tony Waddington asked him about his future, both men knew the answer. It broke his heart, and it broke all hearts for anyone who loved football.

But life went on; Gordon now had the huge mountain to climb of trying to put his life back together. Most people who have had to change career because of some kind of accident do find it a struggle, even people who retire and look forward to a life with their feet up sometimes hanker after their old life. Sometimes it is because it is safe, we know what we are doing, we know what people expect of us, and what we expect from others. One name for this contented frame of mind is institutionalisation, and it is a very positive place to be. The word itself has had its critics, who say that it takes away individual choice, thought and decision, but this is where institutionalisation is a by-product of something else, and not something we often create for our own comfort.

Gordon had many more years left because goalkeepers have longer careers than outfield players. It is difficult to imagine what it must be like turning on a television and seeing someone else doing your job – the job you wanted to do, the job you could do, the job you should have done.

In Gordon's last League game, as I described earlier at Anfield, it finished with Gordon and Mr Kirkpatrick arguing. Liverpool goalkeeper Ray Clemence pulled Gordon away, and soon the two were smiling and the camaraderie was clear. But it was Ray who (partly) replaced Gordon in the England goal; Peter Shilton was also a serious contender and the two shared the job for a while. But how does it feel to see this on television? It must be painful to watch knowing what might have been. I've never got the impression that there was anything but good wishes to his successors, but coming the way it did – early – it must have hurt.

As for Stoke City, they soldiered on, but Gordon was aware of their attempts to sign Aberdeen and Scotland's Bobby Clarke, but this fell through. Again a painful reminder for Gordon of the loss. He has nothing but praise for how his family helped him through the trauma, and it would be fair to say they all worked very hard to get back – to get husband back and to get dad back; they should all be praised.

The defender who rose with Pelé, Tommy Wright of Everton, retired early due to a playing injury, and although this must have been a painful exit, Tommy at least had the consolation that it was on the field of play.

15

Where Do I Go From Here?

In *Banks of England*, Gordon describes his experiences in hospital and how it felt, but facial injuries always look worse than they actually are – blood spilt will always seem a greater volume. One thing that cannot be done by doctors and nurses is to overtake Mother Nature; she has built a robust machine we all occupy, and sometimes when it is damaged it remains damaged. Gordon was to recover from most of his injuries, but the one that mattered most he would have to wait to find if the treatment was to be effective. And again the talent, skills and dedication of the hospital team and the positive attitude from Gordon, still relied on the one thing I mentioned earlier: a heavy slice of luck.

But luck was not with Gordon, and he was left blind in his right eye – the surgeon explained there was nothing more he could do so the damage was permanent.

Tony Waddington had been a tower of strength to Ursula and the rest of the family. He thought Gordon might be able to do a job, but Gordon felt it was the expectations he had placed on himself that were the major hurdles – he couldn't give 100 per cent anymore, it simply was not achievable. Eventually he announced that he would have to 'call it a day'.

As the months rolled on, Gordon took the job of youth-team coach at Stoke, with a special brief at coaching goalkeepers. There was one part-time lad on the books! But it was all a move in the right direction for the profession of goalkeeper because it, again, recognised the uniqueness of the role in the team. He did also coach the rest of the youth team, which was a happy experience.

Lightning, they say, doesn't strike twice, but there can be some fairly loud cracks of thunder in the same general direction. On Christmas Day 1974, Gordon was travelling home after he received a report of a break-in, so he might again have been preoccupied. His car left the road sustaining slight damage, but without injury to him; no other vehicle was involved. The break-in involved the theft of some jewellery and a couple of televisions – none of his footballing trophies were touched.

Stoke City also awarded Gordon a testimonial match, and he describes Eusébio and Bobby Charlton – it might have been more of an honour than first thought – turning out in the same strip as Sir Stanley Matthews.

Gordon's mind turned to coaching rather than playing, but the draw of the gloves and boots were to shout louder. He got the chance in 1976, and he took a few seconds to decide. From the accident and his decision to quit until this time was not the easiest time for Gordon, or the people in his life. But he was to head for America.

Tony Waddington was delighted and assured him that as long as he remained manager of Stoke City, there would always be a job for him.

Most people who have ever aspired for something will usually realise that when they decide they can no longer achieve it, there is a period of grief where they wonder if they could go back and at least mimic former glories. With some it is a disaster, but in Gordon's case the opportunity came for him to return to top-class soccer – top class that is in a country where soccer was not a top-class sport, but it was undergoing some promotion and clubs were looking for former greats to add to their line-ups. So it had some top-class players and top-class facilities, topped with top-class back room staff, and it was to be found in the North American Soccer League (NASL). What it did lack was the Latin American or European passion for the game, but the promoters were doing all they could to sell the idea to the American public.

The 'American Dream' relies on hard work and a sense of daring, so generally their sport is something they are passionate about. But although they had always played soccer, it had not brought out a passion and enthusiasm one could easily identify with other sports – baseball and basketball for example. They had reached the World Cup finals – Alf Ramsey himself had played against them in 1950 when England were beaten. But fourteen years later, Alf was manager of the England team and had selected Gordon for a fixture in New York in May 1964: Gordon was a 'spectator'. One thing is of interest, and that is the description Gordon gives of the facilities – that is to say, the pitch: 'a dustbowl'. Compare this with the description he gave about ten to fifteen years later when the soccer was marketed properly as a family spectator sport: 'every pitch … was like a bowling green.'

He said he loved the football and the standard was far better than he had expected. There were not just stars from Latin America and Europe, there were legends, and Gordon was one of the first. It sounded as though he wanted to show himself as much as anyone what he could do.

The club he joined played in Fort Lauderdale in Florida, and called themselves the Fort Lauderdale Strikers. But before he could play he needed a medical, and Gordon describes the experience superbly in his autobiography. It sounds as though the man with one good eye and limbs that were bolted and pinned together shocked the doctor, but nevertheless he proved he was up to the mark.

It doesn't sound as though the glitz and razzmatazz suited a man used to running out on a soggy pitch in low temperatures, and it also took an age to introduce the players to the crowd. And the heat, even in the evening, was difficult. But as Gordon says, it did give some players an opportunity to play alongside and against big, big names. It also sounds as though a lot of these players lacked one thing in their playing career at home – luck; being spotted by the right scout at the right time.

The Strikers were managed by Ron Newman, who had played professionally in England over a couple of seasons with Portsmouth and a fairly long stint with Gillingham, which sandwiched short spells with Leyton Orient and Crystal Palace. Ron had been a winger – left or right – and when he went to play in America, he took to it straight away. As a manager it sounds as though he knew his football and his players. The Strikers played twenty-six games that season and Gordon pulled the ball out of his net on only twenty-nine occasions – that must have contributed to him being voted North American Soccer League Goalkeeper of the Year. The following season Gordon played eleven games, though the record was not so good. He was asked to stay on in America, but he wanted to return at the end of his two-year contract. He felt the trip had proved he could still play, and he hankered after the English game. In total he played thirty-seven games for The Strikers.

As with other sections of the book, I wanted to discuss performances and I managed to track down some recordings. I'd heard some years before that when television came onto the 'mainstream' in America, they didn't have the points of reference as in UK like, end of part one – commercials – part two and so on. So I started to watch, and in the middle of the action suddenly Karl Malden the actor (*Patton*, *Streets of San Francisco* and more) pops up talking about American Express travellers cheques! It is a bit like seeing an ice cream lady with a fully laden tray come into a church service! Some of the matches I got were only highlights, and a couple were full games, so I can discuss Gordon in a few of the matches.

In July 1977, The Strikers played host to their local rivals, the Tampa Bay Rowdies, captained by former Leicester City great Len Glover, and with Rodney Marsh up front. Gordon had no trouble containing a shot from Rodney, and saved brilliantly from a Derek Smethurst chip just on the 6-yard line – but he was beaten when the former Aberdeen striker, Davie Robb, put in a terrific left-footed shot to Gordon's right that he didn't manage to get to. When there was a stoppage or even a

lull in the action a 'radio' advert was broadcast above the commentary –
McDonalds, a television company and a bank, among others. Gordon did
make a bit of an error with one cross, but the floodlights were not great
which may have contributed. The final score was 3-2 to The Strikers.

On another occasion that year The Strikers were defeated by the
Cosmos ... er ... um 8-3. The goals were brilliant and no criticism
can be made of Gordon. Later, The Strikers were hosts to Cosmos. It
finished all square, but with Franz Beckenbauer, Pelé and a host of other
stars, Gordon needed to be on top form. Pelé was demolished right
on the edge of the 18-yard box; Franz took the free-kick and chipped
it to Gordon's high right – and he did his stuff with a superb save,
which suggested he was still world-class. In his autobiography, Gordon
explains that footballers do not lose their skills as they get older, it is
just that the body slows up. A few minutes later, Franz put Steve Hunt
through and Gordon stifled the attack when a goal looked certain. I
could only get the first half, which had five or six commercial breaks in
it, so it was difficult to follow.

In April 1978, the New York Cosmos were hosts to Fort Lauderdale
Strikers, and the result said little for the defence of The Strikers, the final
score was 7-0. The match was played in quite a strong wind, but the goals
were distributed as three in the first half and four in the second. Gordon
made a couple of saves of note, which I will mention in a minute.

Vladislav Bogicevic opened the scoring in the first few minutes with
a terrific right-footed shot – the defenders just didn't pick him up. Steve
Hunt found most of the left side of The Strikers half was not patrolled by
their defence, and when he got the ball midway between the halfway line
and the 18-yard box, Steve still managed to reach the 6-yard line without
serious challenge for 2-0.

Shortly after, Gordon took a bit of a knock when he collided with
Giorgio Chinaglia. But he recovered only to see Steve Hunt again coming
into his 18-yard box unchallenged to head home Gary Etherington's
cross.

Half time: New York Cosmos three, Fort Lauderdale Strikers nil.

Giorgio Chinaglia was a big striker but very nimble on his feet, and
when Vladislav Bogicavic put him through he twisted and turned, and
went round Gordon for 4-0. And it was Georgio again who shot with
such venom, but this time Gordon could not get down to it in time, so it
slipped under him for five.

The Strikers had some bad luck because when they did have a bit of a
scramble into the Cosmos' half, the ball bounced over Erol Yasin in goal,
and over the crossbar.

The Cosmos' sixth goal was a good passing build-up. Steve Hunt
gained possession in midfield and steered the ball goalward. He passed

the ball between two defenders to Georgio Chinaglia to lay the ball back to Gary Etherington, who squared the ball across for Steve to shoot and score.

The Strikers nearly pulled one back when Roberto Aguirre put in a great shot, but Erol Yasin tipped it over the bar. The corner came over and Erol elected to play it out again for a corner. At the other end, Franz Beckenbaeur nonchalantly sent in a fierce shot that Gordon saved superbly. And Maurice Whittle for The Strikers came close with a shot that was well saved.

Giorgio Chinaglia poached after Vladislav Bogicavic hit the post.

Final score: 7-0.

Later that month, they came up against the Washington Diplomats. The opening credits rolled, and after two minutes the first commercial break aired. The Diplomats had Paul Cannell, ex of Newcastle United, Ray Graydon, ex of Aston Villa and Bobby Stokes from Southampton's triumphant FA Cup-winning team. Gordon didn't get much action. He took one cross comfortably, but was beaten by another that was headed wide. A high cross came over from the right, but Gordon knew it was too high and let it go. The Strikers scored, but the good news ended there really. From a free-kick Gordon picked the ball out of the air, and following the commercial break the action centred on Gordon and a corner. Paul Cannell equalised for The Diplomats. At half-time there had been one goal each for the teams and five commercial breaks!

In the second half, Paul Cannell went close again, and Mike Bakic was just wide with a header. And it was Mike who put The Diplomats in front from Ken Mokgojoa's cross. The Diplomats had the upper hand, and Gordon went off with an injury late on just after their third goal. Bobby Stokes added to their tally, to make the final score 4-1.

A couple of months later, The Oakland Stompers took on The Strikers, who now had Ian Callaghan in midfield. The adverts were as intrusive as ever, and during one early advert the viewer was treated to a replay showing Gordon taking out a low cross. From a free-kick on the edge of the 18-yard box, his stopping was as good as ever; a long-range shot of about 35 yards he managed to put out for a corner.

It was the more entertaining of the three games (total games) I managed to track down. And at some stage David Irving scored for The Strikers!

The second half went from end to end as the midfield seemed to close up shop. Karl-Heinz Mrosko crossed the ball to the far side for Alex Lesh, who sent a fierce shot towards Gordon's goal – but he was equal to it. In the final analysis, Fort Lauderdale Strikers had nearly three times as many goal attempts as The Oakland Stompers. Norman Piper scored their second goal from a penalty. Gordon took out a corner with ease in the last few minutes.

Final score: 2-0.

Between the two seasons in America, Gordon returned to Europe, specifically Ireland, where he played one game for Shamrock Rovers. At the time they were managed by former Manchester United and Leeds star Johnny Giles, and were based in the Milltown area of south Dublin. However, the game he played was away at St Patrick's Athletic ground in Inchicore.

One of the reasons he returned was a broken finger, which meant he would have missed a few games, and with his contract up, the return to family life was a definite desire. Sadly, Tony Waddington had left Stoke City so Gordon was without an appointment. At Southampton, Lawrie McMenemy wanted to introduce a specialised coach for goalkeepers, and when he heard Gordon was at a loose end he made contact. This didn't come about though, partly due to the distance, but also Port Vale were on his doorstep and a coaching job was vacant – and the glove seemed to fit.

16

The Writer

Most of the players associated with the England World Cup campaign of 1966 have written autobiographies, or have had other writers write biographies of them. And in those days, folk of all ages wanted to know all about their hero footballers. But it showed a sad side to many, where everyone wanted to know you one day, but the following day you were yesterday's news. With the coming of the internet, not only have sites sprung up of a 'where are they now' format, but there is more, or easier, access to older books and newspaper archives. And even though it is a fact that the footballer's life is a short, intense one, it is nice to know that they do have (or should I say did have) the same sort of pressures the rest of us have. But modern-day football stars live in a different world, most of the top players earn huge amounts, but the lavish lifestyle this gives them doesn't come cheap. And then there are all sorts of other people in your face, such as agents, advisers and all the rest of it.

With players from the sixties and seventies, many went on to other careers in business, though a few stayed in the game. Alan Ball and Jack Charlton, for instance, became successful football managers; Geoff Hurst and Martin Peters became businessmen; Jimmy Greaves carved a good career on the television; Roger Hunt was in the haulage business; and Ray Wilson, an undertaker.

Gordon went into the business world, but it was not the end of the pleasure he brought, because he also produced and collaborated in a few books, which are well worth a word.

The first volume I could find, by that I mean a book, was one in which he was credited as the editor. *The Park Drive Book of Football* was published in 1968; Park Drive were a cigarette company and in those days cigarette smoking was not criticised as loudly as it is today, and there were a lot more smokers. The book told us that it was endorsed by many footballers who were not smokers, so it is worth looking at it as a book and not think too much about who put up the money for its publication. There were contributions by leading sports journalists of the day, but also footballers and managers. Pat Crerand, Don Revie, Ian St John, Tony Book and Billy Wright, who was in journalism/broadcasting by then, but he was England's most capped player with 105. The best piece in the book was a chapter entitled 'Footballers have Brains', and told the story of the shifting of football from the working-class masses (no doubt stereotyped as 'flat hats and Woodbines') to the more prosperous areas. 'In the old days, you could go to the top of a pit shaft … for a centre-forward. [Now] You would do better to knock the door of a sixth form classroom.'

In 1973, Pelham Books published *Gordon Banks' Soccer Book*; this would have been written and prepared long before the accident. It was a series again of pieces written by journalists and players alike, including Emlyn Hughes, Trevor Francis, Jack Charlton, Tony Currie and Alan Ball – all of whom I'd seen play football – and the BBC DJ, Ed Stewart; a very good goalkeeper!

Gordon's own contributions covered: 'Characters in Football', 'World Cup Soccer and Sir Alf Ramsey', 'Patience IS a Virtue', and 'Bobby Moore – a Great Captain'. It is unclear in what order they were written, so I will just think about them in the order in which they appeared.

But the point I want to make is that they all have their merit, are adequately written and get the ideas across. And also one can pick up the underlying message such as in the first article, 'There Still ARE Characters In Soccer'. The passing of time is a strange phenomenon and one tends to look differently at issues as one gets older, and in this piece Gordon discusses a few of the greats from when he was growing up. Anyone with a particular skill, like footballers with the skill to entertain, tend to stay in the memory. With the coming of wider television coverage of football, the players around Gordon became the next generation heroes, but the 'purity' of folk like Tom Finney, Raich Carter, Wilf Mannion *et al.* is that they were not media superstars with telephone numbers shorter than their week's salary. It was changing when Gordon was at the top, and it has continued to change, and will continue to change. But bring Gordon's list into the next generation, it would not be a surprise to find Malcolm MacDonald, Nobby Stiles, Derek Dougan, Johnny Giles and Billy Bremner on any list of characters. So Father Time's children will mature; Andy Gray, Mo Johnston, Eric Cantona, Graeme Souness. The characters entertained and will go on entertaining. So the piece can stimulate discussion.

The next listed was 'World Cup Soccer and Sir Alf Ramsey'. This was written as England prepared for the Munich World Cup in 1974. Sadly they didn't qualify and this seems to have contributed to Sir Alf's departure as England team manager. This is the best written of the four and is a tub-thumping argument against Sir Alf Ramsey's critics. Clearly Gordon had respect for Sir Alf – and anyone who can lead a club to win the First Division title as a club manager and then the World Cup as national manager has a reputation which precedes them. One thing missing from Gordon's argument was that Sir Alf's 'stern and aloof nature' was often misunderstood.

'Patience IS a Virtue' looks at the delight Stoke City had on winning the Football League Cup in 1972, and they had come close to a Wembley appearance the previous season, only to be beaten in the semi-final of the FA Cup by double-winning Arsenal. He describes well how most footballers put dreams of such success above all other considerations, but underlying this is how second best is better than third best, but far more difficult to cope with.

'Bobby Moore – A Great Captain' looks at the most solid defender of his generation. But also how Bobby conducted himself off the field and the dignity in which he faced adversity. The back four in the World Cup in 1966 were largely marshalled by Bobby and they protected Gordon, though when the opposition did get through, Gordon could more than handle himself. It is not the best written and there is padding, but he gives a good argument and when it comes to summing up and concluding the piece, he does credit to himself.

These are, of course, my own opinions, but Gordon has an elegance to his writing – though he has got the habit of using 'very' to emphasise a point when he makes it quite adequately! The book is more than just a curio, and I'd recommend reading it if you get the chance.

Banks of England was written in the late 1970s and published in 1980 by Arthur Baker Ltd. Gordon registered his thanks to Norman Giller for his help and expertise, but highlights that the book is of the 'greatest era in the history of English football'.

The narrative starts with a description of the accident and how the incidents of the previous day's play when Stoke City were defeated by Liverpool – especially his altercation with Mr Kirkpatrick, the referee – was playing on his mind. He goes on to say that he was at the top of his powers and ability. He reminisces about his boyhood heroes who were all goalkeepers, but his ambitions when he left school, he explains, took him to a coal merchant.

Gordon's life is intermingled with his memory of the situation he found himself in after arriving at the hospital following the accident, and it is cleverly intermingled at that. National Service and his Chesterfield days, and then the move to Leicester City. Then he brings the reader back to the hospital for the news that his sight may be impaired – but as he then goes on to say, Nelson didn't do too badly! Gordon mentions the huge amount of good wishes that came in for him, and how he regretted not being able to answer them all. But life went on for Stoke City, and he concentrated on his health.

Then the realisation came that his sight was damaged and his world was about to collapse. He had his knocks before – his departure from Leicester doesn't sound too confidence-inspiring – but he was to prove they were wrong to sell him. But this was a different struggle. So, as part of his recovery, he put in a lot of extra training to re-educate himself. A goalkeeper is trying to stop a ball coming at him from entering a goal which is behind him. Without eyes in the back of his head, this simple fact shows just how perceptive he needed to be. But Gordon explained that the main problem was the pace of the ball.

As the book develops, it changes course as it looks back over his illustrious career with the England team. At the time of the accident he was the reigning Footballer of the Year and Stoke City were the holders of the Football League Cup.

Overall the book is well written and at times poignant. After the proper *Banks of England* chapter, he describes his life in America and how he felt the Americans would develop as a footballing nation, but it was often a bit too glitzy for the lad from Sheffield. When his contract was up, he'd achieved what he had set out to achieve – he had wanted to prove to himself that he could still keep goal quite adequately, and he could. It also comes across in the writing of the unique role of the goalkeeper in the team – it's almost as though there are ten players plus one.

Gordon puts together his list of 'all-time greats', as well as what he thinks would be the perfect England line-up. There are a few elements to each book one knows the publisher will want!

There is a fascinating end to the book where he has a discussion 'about old times' with Jimmy Greaves. This shows the modesty and humility and above all the 'human' element to the book. The question came up of just how much a sportsman should discuss about his private life – Gordon and Jimmy didn't completely agree but they didn't disagree, and they are entitled to shut their front door. But it's a wonderful discussion and explains why Jimmy didn't play in the 1966 final.

Twenty-three years later, there was another called *Banksy: My Autobiography*. This book was different insofar as it focused on his life as a whole.

He opens with a description of the save he made from Pelé in 1970, and it was interesting to get a commentary from the man. There were other great saves, and that was not his particular favourite, so one can glean that his autobiography was going to be a simple story but one with the fan in mind as the writing took Gordon back to his earliest memories. The opening chapters are divided in what they convey – he paints the picture of a poor artist's home in a poor artist's street, though there is not much of a description of the inside of the house, just the poverty – there was not much in the way of possessions to be had in those days. But he does describe having his weekly bath and getting clean clothes, which is quite intimate; it gives the impression of someone who values the warmth of relationships above material possessions. He was close to his parents and brothers, and it sounds as though he remained so.

His upbringing sounds like many in the immediate post-war era, and he describes how he felt his mum's life was a drudge – but seeing four lads develop and grow is not a drudge to a mother, it can be a pleasure. There was austerity on all fronts, but at least the world was safer now peace had come.

There is a candidly open description of him collecting coal from the local Tinsley steam engine depot, and also of his father's illegal bookmaking; it is difficult to imagine modern-day superstars willing to swallow that much pride.

His introduction to professional football is something he describes to envelop the luck anyone has in this situation, but it does show a modesty and that his best could be improved on if he reflected on his performance and practised – this is a useful bit of advice to anyone in any walk of life.

The story does tend to suffer a bit from his affection for his family and others, but Yorkshire people were not particularly demonstrative in their affections, nor could they describe them – and this comes through; he struggles a bit. Nevertheless, his early years up until his departure from Chesterfield form a 'part one' and being at the top as a 'part two', and most football fans are interested in what happens on the field, so he delivers.

Gordon's description of his years at Leicester give a good flavour of what life was like in the early 1960s, but one gets the impression that the good bits are uppermost in his mind, even at this distance in time. Later, as he loses first his brother and then his father and then his mother, it shows the difficulty he has in describing his innermost feelings – not that different from other folk of the generation.

Turning out in the middle of winter to a pitch like a quagmire to be beaten is all part of the package – winning at Wembley either for club or country in major tournaments is what the reader also wants, so there's a balance. And the behind-the-scenes stories add comedy and drama to make the book worthwhile. What is refreshingly absent is how much booze he could swallow and how wild the life of a footballer is. His affection for some of the players he was friendly with comes through, especially the imps of the game leading him astray – though it doesn't sound as though he put up much resistance. Gordon suggests at least one of his managers was more like a headmaster, and one gets the impression therefore that they all were, at any rate, in his perception. Gordon Banks grew up when 'the chosen' were leaders, and Matt Gillies, Tony Waddington and Sir Alf Ramsey were all good for their players, and his criticism of some of the decisions is, if anything, restrained.

He reached the top and could have stayed there a lot longer, but the way he paints the history of football through the sixties is fascinating; from Pelé to Alf Ramsey, from Jimmy Hill and Derek Dougan through to George Eastham. The World Cup campaigns are dealt with adequately and his affection for the other players, Alf Ramsey and the rock of Harold Shepherdson is clear. The second Geoff Hurst goal in the 1966 final is a source of some irritation because of the doubters, poetically called the 'boffins from the Academy of Rear End Speech'.

He didn't realise the role of pioneer he was creating, and neither did the managers of the First Division at the time. When his departure from Leicester became imminent it was changing, but mainly because of folk like him.

So it was off to Stoke City and his career showed no signs of wilting the way some anticipated – some who should have known better – if anything his career was looking up. In Mexico later he receives news of the OBE. At about that stage in his autobiography he lists some of what he feels are his best saves and accepts global vision will set folk off talking about the Pelé save for generations to come.

The move to Stoke City was a good one, and the friendship he had with Tony Waddington was mutually respectful. To cap it all he describes the joy at being only the second goalkeeper to receive the Footballer of the Year award. This and the Football League Cup win were highlights of the year in which, by a sad irony, his world came crashing down. Suddenly he says, 'I've never liked the smell of hospitals.' The reader knows the end is there. Although Gordon did some coaching and returned to the game, it was more to prove to himself he was still worthy – and America showed him that. I discuss his coaching and management elsewhere; both were disappointments, but players are one thing, coaches another and football managers are a breed apart.

Gordon and football part company, and although he enjoyed life in business, ten years went past in just a few words. He was in partnership of sorts in Leicester, but the company failed in the late 1980s and Gordon seemed to be on the losing side. I say 'side' because he was in a partnership for a motor dealership – he explained that the corporate hospitality company that carried his name was in trouble and went down 'the pan taking a lot of my savings with it' but later on in the paragraph 'a lot of my savings' became 'lost the lot', which suggests two separate issues. I seem to remember one of the so-called consumer programmes doing a feature on a company he was involved with, and their agenda seemed to be to knock Gordon. But I remember thinking at the time that it sounded as if he was taken for a ride – and at the ride's destination he was left carrying the can. He did agree to an open discussion with former clients who felt aggrieved, but lawyers advised otherwise – I don't know the outcome of all this but it seems to me irrelevant here. The reason I think Gordon was as much a victim as others is that Leicester City, nearly thirty years after he left them, offered him a testimonial – I stand to be corrected of any other former player who received this after a long absence from the club.

The FA Cup final attracts huge attention and tickets are valuable – an unscrupulous sort offered some tickets which Gordon later sold. The FA were not happy and gave a prolonged punishment, which was a ban from receiving FA Cup final tickets. It was a ban in which Gordon felt they made to make an example of him, which is against all the rules of natural justice – in natural justice the punishment should fit the crime. Punishments are not written on a walnut with a sledgehammer, some might disagree but his old Sheffield Boys teammate David 'Bronco' Lane would not be one of them.

But Gordon did return to the game, at any rate a return of sorts. The Pools Panel was created to allow the weekly flutter by the public on what the results would be, but if the weather turned against them all would be in vain, so the Pools Panel was created to fill the gaps. Gordon joined some old friends.

With football being so different these days and life for folk growing up is now far less irksome, it's pleasant that nostalgia is no longer considered a sickly sweet wallow in past glories. After-dinner speakers entertain in tuxedos and dickie bows, instead of mud-caked shirts.

Arguments will continue about the best save ever by the best goalkeeper ever. But comparing has its limitations. With the changes to the game – the pitches are now lush, the players more athletic, the tactics and theories and form of the opposition scrutinised more closely, and a greater understanding between the various cultures of the game, i.e. Latin America and Europe – today is a different ball game, if you pardon the expression. It is like comparing a ride in a car on a dust-track to a ride in a car on a motorway. And the ball, while still round, has a different weight to forty-odd years ago.

As I hinted earlier, so many books are written these days about the behaviour of the stars of the game, and most have fairly large sections on their private life, success between the sheets and how much they can drink before they fall over. Some could even write a prison diary sort of book. But in those days, one looked up to footballers, they might have been working-class heroes and football may have been a working-class ballet, but they were still heroes and the magical mesmerising skills they could show were still pretty good, even if most of it was in black and white with the pitches often becoming mud baths after the first couple of months of the season.

But Gordon did eat and drink and had a home to go to at the end of the day, and his family were always the precious element he wanted to enjoy as much as he could. And it looks as though he did, as he and Ursula live in quite close proximity to their three children, now adults with families of their own.

Altogether the 1966 team are still newsworthy. When Bobby Moore died in the early 1990s I remember thinking that people talk about where they were when JFK was hit and when John Lennon was killed; Bobby Moore was as big as them. Alan Ball passed also, but the team regularly hold reunions and charity work also plays a part.

Gordon said he was at the top for the most influential and exiting ten years or so in English football, and all of the writing of all of the players – or whoever graced the page with or without help – is a good commentary of a golden age.

17

Telford United

By the late 1970s, Gordon had made a comeback in soccer and, now he could hang up his gloves, it was further experience he wanted and thought management might suit. He applied for a couple of jobs with League clubs but was pipped at the post by the likes of Graham Taylor. But there was some interest from Telford United, who were a non-League semi-professional side. This didn't mean their application to football and winning was anything short of full commitment, but there were other pressures such as making a living, which sometimes clashed with football. All in all it sounded quite a challenge and in the first week of 1980, Gordon was offered the job of general manager. Alongside him was Ian Cooper as team manager, but although there was no tension between the two, Ian seemed to perceive Gordon's appointment as undermining his own. On the other hand, Gordon seemed to think the two of them could work together and he started to ease himself in.

His 'debut' was away, and to say it was a thrashing would be just about right. Conceding five goals gave him a clear indication where the weaknesses were. He discussed it with Ian, but Ian had called a meeting with the directors, and things started to look more unhealthy for him. By late January, the major concern was one with injuries but there were twenty-six players on the books, which might have been excessive.

Gordon's first autobiographical book, *Banks of England*, was published at this time.

In early February, Ian Cooper resigned as team manager citing his dissatisfaction with the set-up at Telford; he said some of the board members had made life uncomfortable for him. Gordon was still reassessing the squad, but their ninety-minute stints on the pitch were not going well. In the third week of February they suffered defeat number four of four and Gordon transfer-listed five of his players. The side were fourth from bottom of the Alliance League.

By the end of February, the *Telford Journal* could report five new signings and Gordon had finally made his home debut – two months into the job! Three of the players he signed were from Bangor United, and the striker, Dave Mather, turned out to be a good goalscoring forward; he scored three times in his first two matches. The club climbed a couple of places in the League by mid-March, and Gordon was happy with overall progress – a home defeat by Barnet caused some irritation, but by no means a problem.

As Easter approached, the so-called 'Bangor Three' continued in the club's renewed optimism, and Dave Mather's goal tally continued to grow. After the Easter holiday they were climbing towards mid-table, but a couple of defeats made them stumble for a while; they were to end the season a good way from the relegation zone. At the end of the season, six players were put on the transfer list.

In early July, training for the 1980/81 season started and Gordon was looking forward to the new campaign. He was quite happy with the squad and two pre-season friendlies brought Wolverhampton Wanderers and Stoke City who were both triumphant. But it gave Gordon an idea of where he needed some work done – it was in the taking of goals.

The first game of the season resulted in a 4-0 defeat – there was weakness in defence as well as a lack of sharpness up front. A home defeat followed and although Gordon was not too concerned, his concentration was now focused on midfield and was looking for the right player. Gates were falling in number, but September saw the first points start to trickle in; they were bottom of the League but the spirit of the players was high.

Cup games were on the agenda in mid-September and Telford had inadvertently fielded an illegible player in a cup tie (Bob Lord Trophy), so were disqualified. They were also knocked out of the FA Cup. Morale in the team was beginning to flag.

In late September a much more optimistic headline announced 'Pressure eases off Banks after morale-booster'. An away win against local rivals Stafford Rangers saw them jump three places up the League, and Dave Mather was joint leading scorer in the League. But within a couple of weeks it was gloom again for Gordon's men as they had taken only four points from seven games and were second from bottom. Some fans made vocal their feelings that Gordon should be sacked, and some silly goals were being conceded.

October saw them in another local cup game, and Gordon felt the team created chances but just could not finish. Although he was concerned, he was still optimistic. A 1-0 away win highlighted that the defence was settling, but still the strike force was left wanting. Two red cards for two of his players in successive matches was not good news, but Gordon said some of the refereeing decisions in a game at Bath City had been inconsistent. By the end of October, Telford had climbed a bit in the League and things looked promising again.

Injuries were a concern as November arrived and Gordon was forced to make four changes in his team; however, he felt things were beginning to bear fruit and the football Telford played was attractive. They were unlucky away to Boston; they had fought back from two goals down and tried to push forward assertively in the second half. As the bleak November approached December, Gordon's men scored five goals in a decisive victory over Barrow. In December, the report ran 'defence seemed infected by the lethargy of the midfield'. Over the Christmas they conceded seven goals in two defeats with no goals scored.

In January 1981 they were third from bottom again, and had gone eight games without a win. Gordon had gone on sick leave for a hip operation and Jackie Mudie was looking after things. And things continued poorly – Telford had conceded forty-four goals and had only fifteen points from twenty-one games.

A few matches were postponed so it gave Gordon the chance to get on his feet again, literally, before he could get the club back on their feet. At the end of January, they beat Burton United to end their run of losses/draws. The Telford chairman emphasised that Gordon would be back from sick leave though he had a bad bout of flu, which didn't help his recovery. Gordon slammed the press for their speculation of his departure and made his attack to save the players' morale being affected.

They had crept up slightly in the League, but Gordon was thinking about signing an experienced midfielder. In late February they were struggling again and had scored only two goals in a run of four matches.

In March the gloom continued, and they took only one point from five games. Overall, Gordon's record as manager didn't show the improvement he was expecting – in fifty-four games Telford suffered twenty-seven defeats.

Gordon was out and about scouting, as well as looking after things at The Bucks Head – Telford's ground. But the chairman invited him to a meeting away from the ground. With a good few months left on his contract, Gordon was excused from his duties. What followed was a disgrace to football as he was asked to earn his keep selling lottery tickets. It was reported that Gordon settled his differences with Telford United out of court.

18

What if...

By late 1981, Gordon was said to have been 'given the boot by soccer'. He started to tread in the world of commerce by learning the trade of selling insurance, which he said was 'a lot better than the last job I had – selling lottery tickets in the local supermarket'. He wanted to make the best of what life had to offer and not spend too much time on past glories: 'The world does not owe me a living just because I was once a famous footballer.' Now in his early forties, he severed his ties and 'settled out of court' in the wake of his departure from Telford United. Another job in football management didn't appeal.

In the mid-1980s, with the assistant manager of Mansfield Town, John Jarman, the Gordon Banks Goalkeeping Academy for kids was born. The media caught up with him on Mansfield Town's training ground as he passed on the theories of goalkeeping. There was a worry that schools were unable to do as much as they would like, and over the longer term this proved to be the case. Pelé started learning his trade with a bundle of rags, and George Best used to dribble a tennis ball to school and back. Kids would play football in streets, but cars took over. And by the 1980s, signs had appeared barring ball games in the shrinking areas of grass on housing estates. If there was hope it lay with the kids, but where could they learn their trade?

Gordon often played football in the local park (Tinsley Rec), but would also play football under the street lamps.

'Parents won't let their kids out after dark now.'

He said folk in Africa, and he mentioned China too, where there is great poverty away from the commercial centres and children have very little, then there is hope for football, but not so much in the industrialised or advanced nations. It makes one wonder if the term 'advanced nation' and 'sport' is really a contradiction in terms.

In the late 1990s, football was again in trouble and another match-fixing scandal threatened it. Gordon teamed up with Bob Wilson, who was by then a regular with BBC football, to give their expert opinion on the latest claims that games had been 'thrown'. In the spotlight, among other footballers and businessmen, were two leading goalkeepers: Bruce Grobbelaar of Liverpool and Southampton, and Wimbledon's Hans Segers. Gordon and Bob had studied videos of games and their evidence demonstrated they felt nothing untoward had happened. The players were cleared of any wrongdoing.

Gordon lives in Staffordshire these days and because he is still active with the Pools panel, he cannot often get to Saturday games, though when he can he is a regular visitor to Leicester City and The Britannia Ground where Stoke City now play. And he is active on the green grass of the golf course where he has recently teed up with David 'Bronco' Layne, and the day I met him he was trying to recover from the competition of a round with former Leicester City men Richie Norman and Ian King.

He has a touch of arthritis here and there and Ursula is not as well as one would like, but they still manage to get to Germany each year, quite a collection of the family – English branch – go to visit the members of Ursula's family. Their kids are now grown well and there are five grandchildren and a great-grandchild!

Sticking to the football theme of this piece I wondered if, as he was around forty when he went to America, he could have emulated his predecessor as the president of Stoke City – one Sir Stanley Matthews – and carried on playing until he was fifty if the accident had not happened. It brought a glint to his eye and it led me to asking if it might have been possible to return to Stoke City if he could have had more time to retrain himself. He found he had to turn his head when before he only had to glance around. As an example, sit in an armchair and cover an eye, you will see one arm of the chair at a glance but you have to turn your entire head to see the other arm. It might have been possible to return to the game. Also, it was the timing. More might have been achieved in more recent times by the surgeons, eye surgery has advanced, as has orthopaedics; Brian Clough's playing days were ended by a knee injury that both Paul Gascoigne and Roy Keane recovered from and returned to top-class football.

Not surprisingly in his after-dinner speaking he is asked about the Pelé save. Poor old Pelé is asked about his goalscoring everywhere until he comes to England and then he's asked about Gordon Banks. But Gordon still has a passion for football, and when I asked him about some of the managers and if he would have liked to play for them, he wound back the years to discuss some of them. Interestingly, thirty-five years after Brian Clough was snubbed for the England manager job, this still rankles with some former England players. This, together with streets being taken over by cars and signs taking ball games away from town greens, makes another World Cup win less likely. Gary Lineker and Paul Gascoigne *et al.* made the semis in 1990, but that was two long playing careers and a lot of social change ago.

I did want to present a catalogue of his footballing years as the main core of the book, and gave some thought to who should have the last word. I did think that Ian Callaghan as the scorer of the last League goal in the last few seconds of Gordon's last League game should speak last. However, I think he might understand my rationale in bringing in the man who brought both Gordon and Ian into our living rooms. Long before the 'with colour it comes alive', one voice stood out on the BBC as the football man. Barry Davies came along, and then John Motson joined a long list of notable commentators and presenters. But I doubt any of them, or Gordon, would begrudge the quoting of the man who really introduced the schoolboys and their dads (and some mums) to the superstars of the day – Kenneth Wolstenholme. Just before his death in March 2002 he was interviewed for the DVD release of the 1966 final. He mentioned the team members and said of goalkeeper, Gordon Banks:

'He was the best goalkeeper in the world ... he was incredible.'

Index